FIFTY YEARS YOUNG

FIFTY YEARS YOUNG

A tribute to

JOHN B. KEANE

Edited by

JOHN M. FEEHAN

THE MERCIER PRESS

DUBLIN AND CORK

This is a limited edition of five hundred copies.

THE MERCIER PRESS LIMITED
4 Bridge Street, Cork.
25 Lower Abbey Street, Dublin 1.

FIFTY YEARS YOUNG
ISBN 0 85342 579 5

Printed in Ireland by John Augustine Ltd., Dublin

Contents

Introduction

This little collection of essays was put together as a kind of birthday gift to celebrate John B. Keane's fiftieth year. All the contributors are distinguished in their own particular field and their excellent articles give an interesting sidelight on the many facets of this extraordinary man.

I have been publishing the books of John B. Keane for more than twenty years and there is one unique element about this that has struck me time and time again. It is the fact that it does not seem to matter what the critics write about him his books continue to sell in phenomenal numbers. The same is true, I am told, about his plays. No matter how reviewers treat him it does not seem to effect in any way the reaction of the public. And still more strange is the fact that even if literary editors choose to ignore him and not have his books reviewed at all this still does not affect his sales. I do not know of any other Irish author of whom the same can be said.

He is therefore completely unique in the history of Irish writing. The Irish reading public are with him come hail or high water. This is indeed some achievement.

I hope that the study of these essays will open up new paths to the understanding of this strange, mysterious and highly gifted writer.

John M. FEEHAN

The Birth of "Sive"

James N. Healy

The summer was long and hot, and from mid-July to near the end of September there came a succession of sunny and cloudless days. It was the kind of weather which empties theatres and drives those involved on the stage to despair; but not even the weather could beat the phenomenal play which came out of Listowel, for 1959 was the year of *Sive*. It was to be the first production of a new Cork company, The Southern Theatre Group, at the Father Matthew Hall; and while it had become apparent during rehearsals that they had something special on hands few people in the company anticipated the near hysteria which the performances caused or the fact that there would not be a vacant seat in the theatre for six weeks—or indeed, that subsequently they would be performing it in Dublin, Limerick and many other places for almost six months.

The author was a publican in his early thirties. For years he had been writing, generally late into the night after the pub had closed. He believed in himself as a writer but had not had much luck, and by 1959 the belief was beginning to fade. *Sive* had, hopefully, been sent to the Abbey Theatre but had come back with a rejection slip. He had written poetry, but mostly, as it turned out, for his own satisfaction. If in the early part of the year anybody had asked you about the whereabouts of John B. Keane you might have found it difficult to enlighten him but by the autumn there could have been very few people in the country who had not heard of the man from Listowel who had written a play of such fascination. *Sive* had become a cult and it was thrilling enough (even more so in retrospect) to have been caught up in the chain of events. The Southern Theatre Group did not even have a name at that time. It had been planned to do a series of plays during the summer at the Father Matthew Hall with nothing particular in mind and with no plans beyond that. Gradually the idea of concentrating on plays of an Irish nature came about, and one day Dan Donovan mentioned that a man from Listowel had written a play which, performed by his local group, was causing some stir at local festivals. He suggested that as I was producing a musical for the local company in Tralee at that time I might make enquiries. My enquiries in Tralee, over a cup of coffee, confirmed that there was indeed such a play, and such an author, but my young informant advised me: "Jaze, don't go near that fella—he's mad."

He then went on to inform me that the man's favourite trick was to have a metal bar along the front of the counter through which a current of electricity could be passed thus immobilising any client for whom he did not have much regard. I must admit that I cautiously searched for the bar on my first visit there and on other occasions but never found it; and as for his being mad—this is an opinion held by most Irish people about creative persons of their own nationality, and is usually retained until the author is long enough dead to be proclaimed a genius and friend of all.

I drove through the twisting Listowel streets until I saw the sign "Greyhound Bar—John B. Keane". The grocery store was to the front and it was reasonable to assume that the bar was to the back. Behind the counter was a plump young girl who stared at me, when she heard my accent, with the suspicion with which the people of the Kingdom usually treat citizens of Cork. "Whad'da want?" she asked and I tentatively enquired if John B. Keane lived there. She answered, "He do," and made no move beyond that. I said, "Could I see him?" and saying, "I'll get him for you," she left the shop with some reluctance as if she had a wish to count the goods before she left. In a minute or so a narrow face came round the door at the back. Cautiously, silently it observed me through a pair of sharp eyes.

"Whad'da want?"

"Are you Mr. John B. Keane?"

"What about it?"

"My name is James N. Healy. I'm a theatrical producer from Cork.

"I've heard of you." (It didn't sound anything to boast about.)

"I believe you've written a play called *Sive*." (I used the short "i" as in "sieve".)

A short intake of breath.

"*Sive*". (He used the correct pronunciation.)

"I'd be interested in doing it."

"You can have it!" and with that the face disappeared.

After some minutes the girl appeared again—I was still there, shifting from foot to foot.

"Are you still here? Didn't you see him?"

"Er—yes."

"Do you want to see him again?"

"Well—er—" She looked at me but with tightening lip.

"I'll get him for you."

The exit was no less suspicious than before, and then the face appeared again, a little impatient, for he was entertaining friends elsewhere.

"What do you want now—I told you you could have it."

"Yes, well—don't you want to know anything about me?"

"That's all right," said John, "I like your face."

I discovered within a short time that John B. had a way of taking to you or, figuratively, throwing you out the door.

"Maybe," he went on, "'tis the way you want a drink."

It would seem churlish to say no, so I said, "Yes," and entered what seemed a bare, shabby, back-room bar; but it was in reality a kind of Kerry fairyland in which the conversations grew to become the colourful lines of *Sive* and *Many Young Men of Twenty* and so many plays of the next decade. The back bar of John B. Keane's premises was the gathering place for a more colourful set of characters than ever inhabited his plays, and his keen ear had always been there to pick up the phrases and outrageous statements. I was in the birth-place of *Sive* and a number of Kerry eyes whose interesting conversation had been interrupted observed me without comment.

The Listowel Players had agreed to do his play more in hope than expectation; and they had made a good job of it. He told me that it would be on in Listowel the following night. "You'll have to see it," he said. I did and *Sive* did to me what it has done to so many others since—it drew me in to that shabby kitchen and made me live with the Glavins for some hours; for it is without doubt the greatest play to involve an audience that I have ever met. Some of the more literary critics have found faults of construction or probability with the play but nobody could ever question its compelling quality, or the magic of its lines and characters. I contacted Dan Donovan and told him that he must see the play when it went on at the Killarney Festival in a day or so. I also gave John B. a cheque for £50 to secure the performing rights. He didn't know it was the last bit of reserve I had; nor did I know until he told me some years later that it was the best payment he received for anything he had ever written. At Killarney a pattern emerged: the adjudicator attacked the play and the author, with whom he indulged in a verbal battle from the stage. Ernest Blythe, of the Abbey, came up to John B. after the performance and said, "You know, Mr. Keane, I think we might do your play after all." "You're too late," said John, "I'm after giving it to a Corkman!"

Then *Sive* won the All-Ireland Festival at Athlone. Within days the Abbey came through with another suggestion—they invited the Listowel Players to take it to Dublin in June. This presented us with something of a dilemma; we possessed the Performing Rights and were already negotiating with the Gaiety in Dublin; on the other hand we realised what the honour of playing in the Abbey meant to Listowel. We compromised by agreeing that they would go for a week only and felt that this would whet the appetite in the capital for *Sive* without interfering with the business we could expect. However, Louis Elliman, at the Gaiety, told me when he heard of this development that he wouldn't agree to having a "second run". We were lucky that Leo McCabe jumped at the chance of our going to the Olympia, which subsequently became our Dublin home for most of the sixties.

In fact we had included two of the Listowel cast in the Cork production, at John B.'s suggestion—Nora Relihan as the grasping Aunt Mena and Margaret Dillon as Sive.

On the opening night in Cork we were all unusually tense. We were unused to the publicity pressure which had been generated, for press people came from all over Ireland and even from across the water. We just hoped that our performances would match up to it. Perhaps we should let the *Cork Examiner* of the following morning, 26 May, take it from there. "When the final curtain fell on the intensely tragic and moving scene of the old grandmother, who loved Sive, crying out her heart-breaking sorrow, the audience were stunned into shocked silence. Then spontaneously it burst into a thunder of applause. They stood up, they whistled, they shouted; in every way they could they gave vent to their pent-up feelings of delight and appreciation of such a wonderful play and such equally wonderful acting and production". The English papers took it up and one Sunday paper gave a feature page with photos; we had a splendid notice in *The Times*, and even in the *New York Times*. One paper coined the phrase "Theatrical Magic" which we were to use as the play's trade mark.

It is true to say that we, as actors, didn't know what was happening to us—or indeed, in the end, were we able to take advantage of the extraordinary publicity which had been put into our laps; but for the moment all that seemed important was that we were packing the houses. *Sive* was on its way and simply crowded out the other productions which had been planned for the season. It ran the full six weeks.

We became apprehensive all over again as we packed our bags to leave for the Olympia in Dublin—the first Cork company to visit the capital for many a long day, but the reception there was even more than we had bargained for, and again a pattern was being set, for we were to pay regular visits to Dublin during the sixties with each successive new Keane play.

After that we travelled to Limerick, Clonmel, Tralee and many of the Munster towns; it was a particular thrill to walk through the streets of whatever town we happened to be in and hear people whistling the song of the tinkers from *Sive*, which became the hit song of the year.

We returned to Cork and Dublin before, after over a hundred performances, setting the play aside to get Keane's new work, *Sharon's Grave* on the boards. For six years a marvellous succession of Keane plays followed—*Many Young Men of Twenty*, *The Man from Clare*, *The Year of the Hiker* among them. In 1965 our Dublin friend, Lorcan Bourke, who always has had such affection for *Sive* made a request that we would "fill" a week in the Olympia with a revival. We were reluctant as we had been carrying out a policy of doing new plays only but we thought it over and said, "Why not!" It did so well in Dublin that we thought it might run a week or two of our Summer Season in Cork. It ran for nine weeks and, with 54 performances, set a record for the run of a play in Cork which is likely to stand for a very long time.

The Opera House in Cork opened in late 1965 and an excerpt from *Sive* was part of the bill on the opening night. In 1968 there was a full scale revival and once again great houses and enthusiasm. It was obvious that *Sive* had settled in a special niche of affection as far as the public was concerned. In 1972 there came a very special invitation from the O'Growney Branch of the Gaelic League to perform the play in San Francisco and that trip was a memorable one for the company. The performance received a lengthy report in *The Hollywood Reporter* of Los Angeles. It was only later one day when I was in Paramount Studios that one of the studio bosses, Sy Bear, said when I met him "Are you the guy who got this write-up?" and produced a copy of the *Reporter* from his desk. He tapped it with his finger and said, "Do you know that there are top actors here in L.A. who would pay a thousand dollars a line for what you got?" It was only then that I realised what a honour we had received from what is possibly the elite show-biz magazine in the world.

When we first performed *Sive* in 1959 we did, as has been said, feel it was something special, but not perhaps as special as it turned out to be. We didn't think, for instance, that we would still be performing the play seventeen years later in the year of grace nineteen seventy-six which was our last revival to the present date; but *Sive* proved to be different from the laws apparently governing other plays, it created a bit of theatrical history in its own time and, for us, approaching 500 performances, it still carries its own theatrical magic.

Ireland's Lusty Scourge: John B. Keane

THOMAS A. DUFF

THE IRISH respond strongly to the plays of John B. Keane because in them they recognise truths about themselves. Keane has been compared with Tennessee Williams and, like him, has provoked both critics and clergy for his realistic treatment of sexual themes, the rapacity and grotesquery of his characters, and the theatrical excitement his plays generate.

Christy, a night porter at an Irish hotel tells of a guest whose life has become intolerable because of poor health: "I feel so sorry for the man: he's alone; he can't have sex; he wants to die. It's this kind of loneliness that John B. can portray." Katherine O'Sullivan, a pretty nurse at a Killarney hospital, breaks into a wide smile. "John B.! Oh, he's first rate. Very funny. A great character, you know." The mother superior of the hospital adds, "Yes, a remarkable talent; however, I do think that sometimes in his work there is language of a coarser sort."

Like O'Casey and Behan, Keane has received little encouragement from Dublin critics, and from the outset of his career he has been politely tolerated but rarely produced by the Abbey Theatre establishment. But Robert Hogan of the University of California, America's foremost critic of Irish drama, admires Keane's "abruptness and sensuality" and thinks there is no Irish playwright who is "more basically talented" than Keane.

In the south west county of Kerry lies Listowel, a small and ancient farm and cattle town reminiscent of an old photograph sprung to life. The spires of the church of Ireland appear dwarfed and isolated in the middle of the huge town square. Below the hotel window, sinuous and slim, the river Feale streams past. In the distance crows and larks wing the grandstand of the Listowel track, site of the Harvest Festival races each September. During the summer, a writer's conference is held. Downstairs in the lobby, there is a photograph of Keane as president of Ireland's PEN Club, posing with a large group of Irish writers. Listowel itself has produced Bryan MacMahon, author of the story *The Red Petticoat* and the novel *Children of the Rainbow*; the late dramatist George Fitzmaurice; and Eamon Kelly, the great Abbey actor who played the father in the New York production of Brian Friel's *Philadelphia, Here I Come*!

From the square, a winding street to the north leads to a signpost pointing west to Ballybunion and thence to the mouth of the Shannon, nine miles away. It was in this wildly beautiful setting that Maurice Walsh wrote *The Quiet Man*, the John Ford film in which Barry Fitzgerald, *beejees*, oozed enough confection to cloy America about the Irish for a generation.

A few steps beyond the beckoning western road, on the right-hand side of narrow William Street at number 37, stands the pub of John B. Keane. It is a Sunday night at eight o'clock. All the shops are closed and things in this town of 2,500 are quiet. The pub is small and cozy—green cushions and handsome polished wood. The bar itself has room for five tall stools. A door to the left of the bar leads to the Keane home.

This door opens and John B. enters. He is a young, athletic, tall (6′ ½″), and is wearing a bright red sweater, sporty blue slacks and brown shoes. He has a shock of black hair and greenish grey eyes. His manner is animated: everything he says, every gesture he makes is expressed with dramatic energy. He looks like an athlete who might now be a coach or a comic actor. He has acted; but he has also written twenty plays. We shake hands. "You have a good face," he says. We sit down. "I just had a nosebleed a little while ago. I never had a nosebleed before in my life."

"I hope it's nothing serious."

Keane begins to laugh. "Things could be worse," he says, "take your man who owns a store in this locality. He's worth £250,000, but he has a bad stomach, he doesn't drink, and his wife hates sex!"

He motions towards two ten-year-old children who have just come in and are sitting across the room. "You see those girls?" he says in a stage whisper. "They speak nothing but Chinese. It's true." The girls break into giggles. His nine-year-old daughter, the youngest and only girl of four children, enters, sits on his knee and putting her arms around his neck, kisses him. "Now this one," says the father, "speaks nothing but Icelandic. Say something."

"Pryvic ved Fior, Fior," she says. Everyone laughs, John B. especially.

The door opens and several men come in. One approaches our table and silently folds several pounds into his hand. The two men laugh. "Later, sure thing," says Keane. I recall that two of his favourite pastimes are the greyhound races and poker. We have pints of lager. A publican by trade, he frowns upon the use of whiskey. "If a man tells you that he has mastered whiskey you can be certain that it is the whiskey that is talking."

Behind the bar hangs a simple oil painting, depicting a scene from one of his plays. Keane nods, "Yes, the last scene from *Sive*." (It rhymes with "five".) It was the first play he ever wrote. One night in 1959 with his wife Mary, he had gone to see the Listowel Drama Group and, for the first time in his life, was affected by a play. That night, in a nervous burst of energy, he began to write a play of his own. Two weeks later it was finished. He was thirty-one years old.

Sive is a powerful folk tragedy of a young girl of seventeen who fights to free herself from a proposed marriage to Sean Dota, fifty years her senior, and a wealthy, lecherous farmer. Her avaricious aunt, Mena, and Thomasheen Sean Rua, a corrupt matchmaker, frighten her out into the fog and Sive dies an accidental death, drowning in a bog hole. Her body is placed on the kitchen table, her arms folded on her breast. Two tinker musicians deliver a haunting dirge.

Although the theme of the made marriage is not a new one in Irish theatre, the realism of the characters Keane created has a jarring impact upon audiences. The play was an immediate success, winning the Esso award as the best production at the All-Ireland Drama Festival. It was the first of a flow of twenty Keane plays: comedies, folk tragedies, one-act plays, and two musicals.

Keane is one of the few Irish playwrights ever to treat sex openly and with sympathy. In *The Rain at the End of the Summer*, a family is destroyed when the two married sons consider their widower father's desire to marry the housekeeper merely a lustful fancy. In *Big Maggie*, the widowed mother entices a travelling salesman into making a pass at her—knowing that her daughter, who is flirting with him, will discover them embracing. She crushes the budding romance so as to keep the daughter as an employee in her shop. In *Sharon's Grave*, Dinsey Conlee, a crippled hunchback who uses his brother Jack as a horse, explains his longing for a woman: "I would polish and shine her shoes for her like the black of a crow's wing. I would cut her toenails and wash her feet for her in the evening."

In each of these plays and several others Keane articulates the unspoken needs of man for love. Once asked if sex was a symbol for the entire human state, Keane replied, "Yes . . . There was and still is a dreadful attitude toward sex in rural Ireland. It was the only unmentionable admission. Men and women concealed the fact that a physical longing existed. It was seen as something to be ashamed of."

We have a second jar. He is inquisitive. "What do you think is the strength of my work?" he asks.

"As plays, their variety, movement."

"It's the characterisation. The people of Kerry say my characters are authentic, and I write for them, not the critics in Dublin."

"And aren't you criticised for being too local, too provincial? The same kind of thing that Frost and Faulkner were criticised for?"

"A man belongs to where he is. If I belong to Listowel, I belong to Ireland, and if I belong to Ireland I must belong to the world. To be parochial is to be universal. Isn't this what Dylan Thomas shows us in *Under Milk Wood*?"

Other traditional themes of Irish drama are found in his works: lust for land and money, family conflicts, social climbing, and emigration: "Themes don't really change but they do evolve. I am so near as to be part of what happens in my plays. Consequently, the plays are significantly more realistic than others which have dealt with similar themes. For instance, in *The Field*, which is drawn from an incident which took place near the country house where I was reared as a boy, I use some of the actual principals involved in the incident which, incidentally, is indigenous to rural Ireland, that is: murder arising from lust of land. I think it is most significant, in view of the violence in the North of Ireland and the reputation that we Irish have for violence, that an Irishman will kill for land or for an ideal but never for love of a woman. *The Pure of Heart* deals with a man who will kill a fellow human being rather than commit adultery.

These values are worth examination, are worth highlighting if we are to honestly know ourselves as a race of people."

"What is your best play?"

"Have you read *Crazy Wall*?"

It is the story of a husband who neglects his wife and two sons to build a stone wall which will make him famous and keep his name alive after he dies. It is a symbol of a man's wordly concerns, the artist's work—that which may sever him from his family? I remember a passage from Keane's *Self-Portrait*:

"I would begin at twelve o'clock at night when all the customers had departed. I'd fill a pint and draw the table near to the fire . . . and I would write till three or four o'clock in the morning."

"I went through a crisis in my life five years ago. When I was 42."

"Do you still write late at night?"

"No. Only in the mornings now. I have found the most important thing in my life."

"What's that?"

"My family."

John Brendan Keane was born in Listowel on 21 July 1928, fourth in a line of nine. He had four brothers and four sisters. His mother was the daughter of a small farmer; his father a teacher of the fifth-grade in the Listowel National School, who later became principal of Clounmacon National School, three miles away. His father introduced Keane to the gallery of characters in Dickens and Shakespeare, his favourite authors to this day. It was during his summer holidays in the nearby Stack's Mountains of Tralee, however, that he "for the first time met characters who mattered and people who left a real impression."

Keane remembers his high school years with loathing. St. Michael's in Listowel had no teams, no athletics of any kind. He was expelled several times: for smoking, speech making, and strangely, for acting and writing poetry. His decision to become a writer was made at this time. Unlike Joyce's vision of loveliness, Keane's career began with a beating by a teacher. Called upon to recite a poem in class, he chose one of his own poems called "Church Street", a simple 24 line lyric about the street on which he was born. Although no explanation was ever given, the teacher was probably outraged by his "audacity" and thrashed Keane severely. From that day on he wanted to write.

In September, 1951 Keane met Mary and they fell in love. Now 22, with no prospects in Ireland, he made a decision that 50,000 other Irish made in 1952: emigration. He chose England because it was closer to home and Mary. Joyce and O'Casey fled into exile to escape, but some of the strongest moments in Keane's work are based upon his sorrow in leaving Ireland and are typical of Irish who have fled their country through the years.

"All around us as we left Dún Laoghaire there was drunkenness . . . Of all the things I've ever felt or seen, nothing ever so moved me as the sight of these men and women being torn away from home. If you want to laugh now is your chance . . . you'll be heard by some lonely old couple whose loved ones are lost forever . . . I have been accused on several occasions of highlighting the problem of emigration and of evading the issue of a solution. The solution is —don't go. Stay at home."

Self-Portrait, 1963

Keane worked in a variety of menial and labouring jobs in England. Lime Street Station in Liverpool, the grim skylines of Northampton and London's Camden Town, the squalid quarters and the wretched food engraved themselves upon his imagination. He felt the loneliness, the penury, the despair:

Oh Cricklewood, Oh Cricklewood,
You stole my youth away,
For I was young and innocent,
And you were old and grey.

This was a song sung by the buck navvies, Irish working men in England. Keane's plays are dotted with songs. In his highly popular musical, *Many Young Men of Twenty*, the barmaid Peg, soon after the play opens sings:

Many young men of twenty said goodbye
All that long day.
From break of dawn until the sun was high
Many young men of twenty said goodbye.

The men left Ireland because they had no opportunities for work, but it is clear that Peg is stranded because of the fear and disgrace her young lover

Jimmy felt in fathering her child out of wedlock. There are searing attacks upon parents who regularly deposit their children at depots in anticipation of receiving a "fiver" from them every pay-day when they find work elsewhere. Keane is no sentimentalist here; he aims to examine motives and to plant scruples. "England is no place for the underschooled unattached boy or girl of eighteen to twenty-one," he maintains. "If England is to be the lot of these impressionable adolescents, it should be the lot of their heartless fathers and mothers too."

Keane began to write a novel without success, and after a stint as a street sweeper, took a job in the hardening shop of British Timken, an Anglo-American steel company in Northampton. His novel and a second one were rejected, as were stories, essays, and poems. He speaks with great joy of receiving a first cheque for £15 from a women's magazine, the money from which was promptly splurged in London the following Saturday night. He finally returned to Ireland, and after a year's work at a shop in a small town, bought the pub in Listowel which he and his wife still manage. Back in his native town, he spent the next two years serving the public, a job he did not especially relish, yet one which provided him a continuing source of income, anecdote and speech. Then he began to write again. "I look to life as it is lived around me, and listen to the language that is living. People need to be recorded, to be witnessed."

The pub is now crowded. We get up from our table and he goes behind the bar. "Hello, Pat," he says to one of his customers. "Ah, only your solid man smokes a pipe. You're the most contented man in Ireland." The two men begin to talk.

Keane's theatre is full of hope. It celebrates life and love with great humour and vitality. It warns against the dangers of denying the integrity of the human heart and its basic needs: reassurance, faith and love. His plays are the very words and life of his people. He is their conscience and they love him for it.

The Short Story Teller

BRIAN CLEEVE

A GOOD SHORT story is like a good tune. It dwells in the mind. Not too long to be easily memorable, nor too complicated; not too short nor too simple to allow for developments, and subtleties, and make it worth rehearing, or rereading, or letting run through one's mind again. It will even grow in the mind, taking on virtues and colours that the original scarcely seemed to possess on a first experience. One or two of John B. Keane's short stories are of this kind, and I hope John will not be angry with me for what seems at first sight like faint praise. "Good"? rather than "magnificent"? "One or two"? rather than "All"? Birthday volumes are not usually the place for analysis, and weighing of words. Rather they call for after-dinner compliments, and the singing of "He's a jolly good fellow." And I shall gladly add my share to the compliments, and my cracked voice to the chorus. But I should like to add something more, and give John my own personal birthday offering of truthfulness. So, I stick to "good", and "one or two", and to my mind this is already a tremendous compliment. How many short story writers in Ireland, or anywhere, have written any stories that really dwell in one's mind, long after one has read them? Very few. I have read my share of short stories over the past many years, and I remember, *really* remember, a bare half dozen, if as many as that. Two or three by de Maupassant, more uncertainly one or two by Maugham, two or three more by writers whose names I've forgotten. And now at least one of John B.'s, *Death be not Proud.*

If you have not yet read it, it's a very simple story, on first reading. An old farmer wants one of his sons to follow him on the farm. He is left with the least likely candidate, a lad who ran away to England years ago, and has worked in a car factory ever since. He persuades him to come back, and they get on very well together. But the old man is not yet certain of how deep the younger one's feeling is for the land. It is enough, but is it like his own, as deep rooted as a thorn tree? In the climax the mother is helping gather in the hay. She has already suffered a heart attack, but they are short handed and the men helping are not much use. There are only a few hours of good weather left, the rain is coming. She begins helping, suffers another stroke, and dies, with her husband beside her, in a far corner of the field. The two labourers are a long way off and unaware of what's happened. The son, who is driving the tractor, makes his long circuit and comes to his father kneeling beside the mother's body. The son gets down, sees what has happened, and kisses his mother's lips and forehead, settles her head on a pillow of hay. Then he rose, and looked at the sky.

"'Let's get on with it," he said. At first Mick Henderson looked at him uncomprehendingly. Then the logic of it dawned on him.

"What about the two?" he asked, pointing to where the labourers were building a cock at the other end of the meadow.

"What they don't know won't trouble them," said Mikey dismissing the question. Slowly his father rose. Already Mikey was adding to the half-made cock. Instinctively his father followed his example.

Before departing for another rake-up Mikey laid a hand on his father's shoulder.

"She would understand," he said. "I don't have to tell you that. When the job is done we'll take her indoors. Then I'll go for a priest.'"

He goes off on another round of the field, raking in the hay with the tractor, and his father watches him for a moment, saying to himself, "Beyond doubt here was a man with a sound sense of values, a man with a true feel for the land."

Now, you can share that sentiment, or find it horrifying, but you can't dismiss it, or forget it. As I read the story, those last paragraphs gave me the jolt one gets walking into a tree in the dark. This is reality, the bedrock of human nature, one kind of human nature, and John B.'s genius is to take just such a lump of raw, real humanity, give it a rough smack with his hand, and say "there, look, take it or leave it, but that's the way things are." Indeed, I don't think he says even so much as that. He just puts it in front of you, and lets you do the rest.

I said genius, and not talent or skill, and I meant it,

and not as an unadulterated birthday compliment. John is a playwright before he's a short story writer, and perhaps he's a poet before he's a playwright. The few short stories of his that I've read strike me for the most part as a playwright's notes, for plays he has not yet written; as a fine artist might make pencil sketches before he reaches for his brushes and palette. He is not too much concerned to make them finished things in themselves, but rather to work out an idea sufficiently to see what way it might serve him in another medium. But if a man has genius his most casual sketches will bear the stamp of it, and reading *Death be not Proud* I felt the same shiver of excitement at the ending as I felt long ago when I first saw a production of *Sive* in Dublin. Here I felt, then, was a man with something real to say; not the kitchen sink realism of too many stale plays, and flaccid playwrights, but the deep realism of a man who knows that life has mysteries in it, and who knows how to listen for their footfalls in the dark.

It is exactly this sense of mystery, of depth on depth and under depth of reality that I myself look for in any work of art; painting, music, play, novel, short story. A sense of death and unknown things behind the curtain. The story may be comic, or tragic; the curtain may hang in a city drawing room, or be formed by grey mist on a hillside; the mystery can still be there. And it is there in John B.'s work, and for me gives it its deepest value. But of course it has another value as well, and it too is part of that mist on the hillside. Because John's work belongs to the Kerry hills like the gorse and heather.

A long time ago Daniel Corkery took a great swipe at what was once called "Anglo-Irish writing", which means broadly the books and plays and poems written by men and women who live in Ireland but write in English; Corkery took a flying kick at all of it, from Maria Edgeworth to Yeats, and said that it had no right to the word Irish; that the only Irish writing was that done in the Irish language, and that the rest was unnational. But he made one exception, for John Synge (and perhaps another for himself, since he too wrote most of his work in English) and I think if he was revising his book today he would make yet another in favour of John B.

Because John B.'s work is not only Irish, and in that sense national, it is local. It belongs to his countryside as the rocks do. And yet in spite of that, or perhaps because of it, it could be understood by anyone who knows and loves any countryside, even if it was on the other side of the world. Any farmer, in Australia, in Russia, in South America, in France, could understand the feelings behind the story *Death be not Proud.* Or in another of John's stories which I almost think—which on reflection I do think—I prefer to it, called *The Reek.*

Two ancient brothers possess a slice of bogland where each year they cut and stack their turf for fuel. Everything connected with the turf is a ritual and an art, from the way it is cut from the bog, to the way the stack is built by the roadside, to the way the cutters take their rest and their meals sitting on the grass, and the donkey is loosed to take his own refreshment "of good grass and wild clover". The least detail is of importance, not because the men concerned have thought the matter out, but because such things have always been so, and any change must be for the worse. While they are eating their midday bread and meat, for example, they are discussing townspeople who had recently begun to invade the boglands and cut turf for themselves. "I seen strange things," one of the turf cutters says, "but I never before seen the likes of these men. They had bread with meat in the middle of it. You could only see the edge of the meat. The rest was covered by bread above and below. There is no way you could inveigle me to eat meat I couldn't see."

The story is set during the last war, and everything about it catches not only the place, but the time. It *is* a summer's day out of the 1940s, caught like a golden butterfly, and set in amber. The colours of the bog, the stillness of the late summer afternoon, the smell of that good grass and wild clover, of the pools of bog water, tawny dark and mysterious; and above all the shape and the feel of the reek that one of the old men builds with the artistry of the men who built the great passage graves five thousand years ago; shaped and shouldered against the wind to stand for ever, justly rounded, justly aligned, perfect. It is a work of art, and recognised as a work of art, a masterpiece, by all who see it.

The two old men go back to their cottage, and the reek builder dies that same winter of pneumonia. His brother does not use the reek of turf for fuel, but keeps it as a memorial, and for three years it survives winter storms and summer heat, bleached by sun and rain from dark brown to a frosty grey, until "On clear nights, under an unshrouded moon, it seemed as if it was a great rampart of silver."

There seems no reason why the reek should not outlast the surviving brother until it becomes a grass grown mound by the roadside, a true memorial for ever. But that next spring a band of tinkers comes by, with a flock of mongrel dogs and children and three multi-coloured, horsedrawn caravans, and although the old man watches them hawk-eyed the children distract his watchfulness long enough for their elders to filch sods of turf from the reek, leaving gaping black holes and cavities along the side nearest to the roadway.

Nor is that the end of it, for the tinkers decide to camp in the bog, and nothing is more certain than that they will make deeper inroads into this tempting stack of perfect fuel, dried by a dozen seasons so that a sod will catch light in the fire like a billet of old timber. But if the turf is now perfect for burning, the reek is ruined. Once its smooth-built exterior is broken and gapped like this the rain will get in, the wind will tear at its innards, and within a few more weeks of storm there will be nothing left but an oozing hillock of mud.

And so the old man takes a bucket full of embers from his kitchen fire, and places them carefully in the base of the reek. "For the freshening breeze it was a labour of love to achieve the rest."

I think, I know, that this is a story that will live with me as long as I remember any stories, and that each time I think of it again, or reread it, I will find something else to be happy about, or that has a meaning I had not yet discovered. As I said at the beginning of these pages, it is like a good tune, not too long nor too complicated to be remembered, nor yet too short, nor too simple. There is only one place in the world that it could have happened, and only a year or so in the whole stretch of man's history, and only a day or so in those years that could have given birth to it. Yet effortlessly, the story expands this brief moment and this small space until it has immense significance, spreading out into the great events of the world outside, and reaching far back into the past, beyond history, with that invasion of the dark and silent band of tinkers, nomads out of an unknown past. "Elsewhere the fate of the world was being decided. Far away in Cairo, Churchill and Roosevelt were meeting with Chiang Kai-shek and in southern Italy fierce battles were raging as the Allies endeavoured to advance northwards."

A neighbour called Hanafin possesses a radio, which tells them of these things if they care to listen, and also offers them forecasts of the weather, which the wiser of the two brothers disbelieves, preferring to trust the feel of the wind. "The wind is from the right point and there's heating in it and if there's heating in it then by all the laws the sun will be along after the wind."

There is no traffic on the road, because it is war time, but this does not need to be said. There was simply no traffic; as simply and immutably as the fact that the sea lay five miles away. The donkey rolls on his back in the dustry road. *He* knows that no lorry will come thundering past to frighten his life away. And *this* does not need to be said. John B. leaves it to the reader to discover these things for himself, like the taste of those great wedges of home made bread and home cured bacon that the turf cutters eat for their leisurely midday meal.

And there is the brief-sketched humour of the townspeople, brief, yet deep with levels and under levels of meaning; the townsmen "racking their hair before futting the turf. I have seen them and they wearing low shoes only fit for dancing and they trying to operate a slean."

There is the hard-headed country realism of the one brother watching the other sauntering down the road, still "erectly if somewhat irresolutely". "There's a stagger to him," the brother whispers. "I knew what this meant. A stagger was taken to mean that a man was nearing his end, maybe not immediately nor for a considerable time It was a telling factor, however, from which there was no reprieve."

Yet this is the brother who mourns in such fierce silence for his dead companion.

And finally, or no, not finally, for I expect for a long time to come to find more things to remember and treasure and savour in this story, there are the tinkers. That wild, soft-footed band of marauders, the children and the mongrels playing along the road in front of that "swift-moving but silent caravan", and "the faces of the menfolk who led the caravan horses . . . blue with cold". Where did they come from? Where were they going? A thieving, piteous savagery, frightening and frightened, hunched against the

March wind, the lingering breath of winter The echoes come crying out of the dark and vanish into it, and the reek goes flaring up like a funeral pyre.

Yes, I shall remember this story of John's for a long, long time, and I thank him for it, and wish him another fifty years of story-telling.

John B.

Ray McAnally

There's bonfires on the hillsides,
There's cheering in the glen,
John B. is celebrating
The two score years and ten.

Twenty years of poetry,
And twenty years of plays,
And a new book on the market
Every ninety days.

The world keeps singing in his ear
And dancing for his eye—
He gathers it and stores it;
It'll ripen by and by.

And when the moon has canopied
A world of dreaming men,
John B.'s awake, remembering,
And reaching for the pen.

And Matchmakers and Parish Priests,
Big Maggie, Thady, Sive,
Bull McCabe, Fionnuala Crust,
It's then they come alive.

Has he bugged the brains of Paradise?
Has he tapped the angels' phone?
Has God the Father special gifts
For John B. Keane alone?

God the Son is worried
With a sense of cosmic guilt
Because he hears in Heaven's halls
The dancing Kerry lilt.

"Almighty Da," he says, "You know
The secrets of the soul.
Is the Holy Spirit biased
In favour of Listowel?

An awful thought has struck me,
Almighty Da Serene—
Is the Holy Ghost a Kerryman,
Or is He John B. Keane?"

An Irish Rabelais

Des MacHale

To my mind John B. Keane is one of the handful of genuinely comic writers that this country has produced since the turn of the century. True, he is also a dramatist, poet, short story writer, and columnist, to mention but a few of his talents, but his most precious gift is his natural sense of humour and his rare ability to transmit laughter through the sombre medium of print. One is continually reminded of Rabelais, because Keane's humour has an honest-to-goodness attitude to what might loosely be termed coarseness and vulgarity. Yet, the treatment of these delicate topics is always sensitive and I have yet to meet anybody who has been offended by his writings. Keane's humour is firmly rooted in reality, and in rural Ireland he has not far to look for the characters he delineates, because God knows the countryside is teeming with bicycle-clipped postmen, gombeen T.D.s, frustrated chastitutes, spinster postmistresses, scheming matchmakers and pre-Council of Trent parish priests that could have stepped straight from his pages. He has little time for erudition, sophistication and multilingual punning in his writings because they are as unnecessary as Japanese subtitles. Keane's humour is the authentic reflection of the lighter side of the life of his fellow countrymen and by any criterion, this is surely what good humour is.

All of which brings us to his *Letters*. Keane of course is not the first Irish humorist to have used the Letter both as an instrument of satire and a wedge to expose the idiocies of life and society in these islands. In fact, the Letter so used evokes the memory of the caustic wit of Swift in the Drapier Letters and also the more gentle but no less effective satire of Goldsmith's *Letters from a Citizen of the World* and Suzanne R. Day's *The Amazing Philantrophists* written in 1916. Ms Day (for I know not her marital status, and a fellow cannot be too careful nowadays with all those militant females about) wrote a series of episodes in Letter form concerning the life and times of one, Lester Martin, Poor Law Guardian of Coomacronia, Ballybawn. Martin was a sort of Anglo-Saxon gombeen man, politician and commentator on the colonial Ireland of his day and not too unlike Tull MacAdoo, the successful T.D.

John B. has made the Letter virtually his own property in the field of Irish humour. I wish by the way there was a better word than the anaemic "humour" to describe his funny writings—something with a nuance of impish cunning with overtones of good natural ribaldry, but perhaps it is too much to expect that any language, especially English, would possess such a word. A phrase of a relative of my own might possibly come closest to what I have in mind—"read a paragraph of Keane's and," as she would say, "you'd know that the Devil himself was a-riding up on the fellow's back".

The Letters have flowed from his pen in a seemingly endless stream. Parish Priests, Postmistresses, Publicans, Matchmakers, Postmen, Gardai, Farmers and T.D.s have all come under fire and none has escaped Keane's barbed ire. His Letters speak for themselves through their writers. Hopefully, we can expect that he is now in full flight, because the stock of Irish prototypes is by no means exhausted. Surely Keane has yet to divulge the intimate correspondence of the Irish Nun, the Trade Union Official and the Irish Publisher. Will he deny us the Letters of the Family Planner, the Poteen Maker, the Irish Feminist, the Civil Servant, the RTE Producer and the National Teacher?

A full analysis of Keane's humour would be lengthy and say more about Ireland than any ponderous thesis in sociology, so in this short tribute I will concentrate, quite properly, on those writings of his that make me laugh the most. His funniest material, in my opinion, is all below the belt, both literally and figuratively and yet there is no full frontal stuff. To coin a phrase, Keane's humour is back frontal and nobody since Rabelais and the renowned La Petomane has squeezed so much laughter from the natural functions. Listen to the following analysis of Father Bosco McNelly addressing himself to the folk of Tooreenturk proper but in particular to the scoundrel who had relieved himself at the entrance to the church on the very day of the Bishop's visit:

> "Let me say," said he, "that I take no exception to a man relieving himself if he is caught short. I have no objection to a sick person who cannot restrain himself but," and here he was vehement, "I had a good look at the heap outside the door of this church, and I can safely say that it was the result, not of a sickly misfortune but of a mighty strenuous effort.
> The Bishop who was a sensitive man made a mental note never to attend at any ceremony in the parish of Tooreenturk until such time as Bosco had departed from it."

Students of physics will note that Keane covers all three states of matter. In his Essay on *Calls of Nature* we learn that

> "In Listowel up until a few short years ago there was a man who used to climb trees in order to relieve himself. God help an unwary passer-by and a thousand woes to him who upon hearing a rustle overhead felt obliged to gaze upwards."

In *Unusual Catches* the fisherman's most mundane bag is transformed into a hilarious scooping of the pot—it all depends on the way you look at it, I suppose:

> "In the book of records Dandy Keane was credited with landing the largest enamel chamber pot ever to be hooked by rod and line from one end of the Feale River to the other. I have no idea how many gallons it would contain but under the entry ran the following description: *Chamber Pot. Enamel. Perforated at bottom. Handle*

> *attached. To hold water of twenty.* No mean achievement this when one looks at the puny, pint-sized, plastic chamber pots of today."

The time honoured custom of the breaking of wind which is as old as man himself, is a favourite topic of John B.'s. This following paragraph should help to complete everybody's education concerning this most fundamental subject:

> "Everybody breaks wind. There are some who pretend they don't but the fact remains that we cannot always harness the tumult that thunders in the anus after unwise consumption of excessive food and drink. There are certain ladies whose fragile and angelic features would suggest that they are above such a lowly practice but, believe me, like truth the wind will out no matter how hard they try to suppress it."

Indeed, a vital development in the plot in *Letters of a Country Postman* is provided by the breaking of wind:

> "One night they coaxed a Spanish colleague into making a phone call to Katie announcing that he was the new Papal Nuncio, Doctor Elbrigandi. Katie burped in surprise into the mouthpiece to be informed in broken English by Doctor Elbrigandi that she was being excommunicated for farting."

The humour of Keane's essays is quite different from the stinging satire of his Letters. It is not to belittle them in any way to say they remind us of the essays of another great Irish humorist John D. Sheridan. Keane's essays are a fine rural counterpoint to Sheridan's stouthearted apologia for suburbia which he subtitled "A Defence of the Aspidistra", but a glance at some of Keane's titles such as *Goose's Blood*, *Spare Ribs*, *Garters*, *Pudding Filling* and *Butt Sucking* shows that he deviates little from his earthy themes.

It has been said that the best humour is merely a subtle portrayal of what happens in everyday life. If this is the case the humour of John B.'s essays is of a very high order indeed, because he has a fine eye for spotting the eccentricities of rural Irish life. I find that it is single sentences of his that linger in the memory for months or even years afterwards rather than whole essays and indeed sometimes a whole essay is worth reading for no other reason than that it may contain a gem like one of the following:

On Corns: I once knew a woman who wore out three bicycles in search of a cure for corns.

August Thoughts: There are many intelligent people who believe that Shakespeare was really a Kerryman who left Ballybunion after the disastrous August week-end of fifteen eighty.

On Garters: Garters played the part of guardian against incursions above the knee. The garter was the timberline of morality and the plimsoll line of security. Can the same be said for tights?

On Bucket Handles: I was entering a hostelry in Killarney when I was approached by a man who accused me of never having written about bucket handles.

John B. Keane

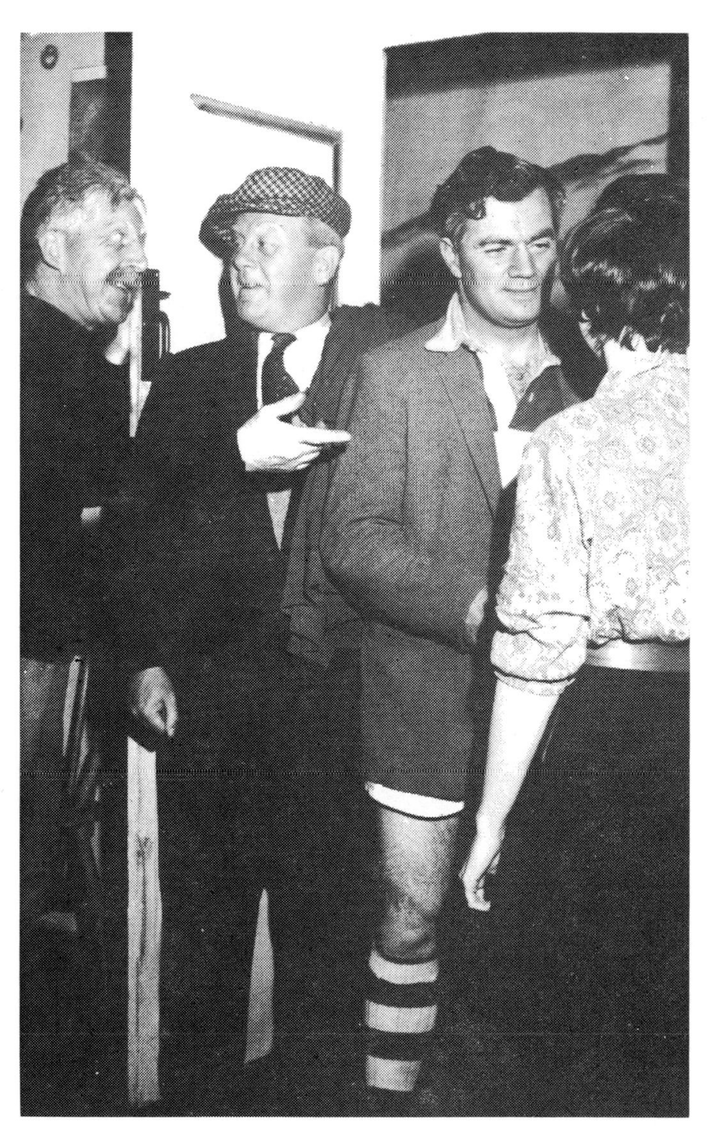

'The Man from Clare'

John B. Keane's *Self Portrait* is as honest and touching an autobiography as one could read. His early life was a struggle but he believed in his own ability to write and eventually made a break through with a new approach to Irish drama. His humorous writings came later when he had settled down and found relative security after his return to Ireland. The best humour is usually firmly based on real life happenings and it is interesting to speculate just how much of Keane's later comic writings may have been inspired by the experiences recounted in his *Self Portrait.* For example, there is a familiar ring to the NOTICE TO GUESTS displayed in his English digs:

> "Guests will not use chamber pots, bed pans, urinals or commodes in bedrooms. Guests will not keep cage-birds, dogs or pets of any kind. Guests will not entertain female visitors. Guests will not spit while indoors. Guests will not bring alcoholic drinks into bedrooms. Guests will flush toilets immediately after use.

I once translated it into pidgin English for Joe the Pole No. Two. He had always believed it was a house blessing, and he took a dim view of the Atkinsons thereafter."

The hilarious invention of the fictitious politician Tom Doodle and his ensuing exploits during the 1951 General Election campaign are a good indication of Keane's use of the prolonged practical joke, another Irish tradition of long standing. It is a pity that he has not given us more of this type of exploit, either real or imaginary in his writings. However, by far the funniest incident recounted in the *Self Portrait* is the real life, after-hours encounter between the publican and the guards on duty. This scene has all the ingredients of pure comedy and I would love to see it expanded into a short story or a farcical one-act play:

"Anybody on the premises?"

"Devil a one, Sergeant!"

"Is there anyone upstairs?"

"There's two or three, Sergeant!" There might be anything from forty to a hundred up there.

"I'll go up," the Sergeant would say.

"Yerra, don't bother, Sergeant. I'll go up and bring them down for you!" Upstairs, some of the boys were in bed with their clothes on. Others hid in wardrobes, or under beds. The toilet was crammed to capacity and the door locked from within.

"There's a raid on, lads," I called. "How about a few volunteers?" A moment's pause and three men came forward from their respective hiding-places.

The finest compliment that one can pay to any comic writer is to acknowledge that the reading of his books causes loud, frequent and uncontrollable laughter, and this is the effect that John B. Keane has on me and thousands of other readers. The great comic novel of the century in the Irish Language, *An Beal Bocht*, has already been written. I believe that Keane is the man to write the great comic novel for which the English language is crying out. Only an Irishman can write it of course, so how about it John B?

Plain Man of Poetry

CHRISTY BROWN

WHEN IT WAS suggested that I might like to write something as a small tribute on the occasion of John B. Keane's fiftieth birthday, I agreed at once, only too happy to add my own weak voice to the concourse that will no doubt descend upon his honoured cranium to mark his fifth decade among us. So I set to with a will and grandly headed my article: An Appreciation. It was only after several paragraphs that I realised the appalling inappropriateness of that heading, since it is usually synonymous with an obituary, and as far as I could recollect—certainly from a most recent convivial encounter with the individual himself—I was writing in order to praise and not to bury this particular warrior. Hence some feverish rearrangement was most urgently called for to dispel any misapprehension that I was about to sound the Last Post over his hypothetical corpse at a moment when he was most likely engaged in either one of his favourite professions: pulling pints, writing plays, or talking. I believe it has been known that he has invariably done all three at one and the same time, but then he always has been something of an exhibitionist—one of the nicest ones around in this or any other age.

I also faced the usual problem about writing in cold inanimate print about a friend whom one has known for many years and saying things that would not come across sounding stilted, deliberate, precise and devoid of spontaneity, as is usually the case with all but the most polished—I was tempted to say hardened—essayist. It is so much easier to exchange opinions, pleasantries and amicable obscenities over a couple of pints and a ball or two of malt in a congenial corner of a snug, but it is altogether a different and far more fearsome task to sit crouched over your typewriter for hours wondering what the hell you are going to say that will sound even half way sincere or marginally interesting to those who will—hopefully—eventually read it. You may end up nursing a profound grievance against the machine itself for remaining so obdurately silent and refusing to offer a tincture of help or advice to assist you out of your little dilemma. There was also another and quite separate quandry in that although I have known John B. over several years, I am by no means what might be termed "an intimate" of his; that is, we do not meet each other on a week to week, month to month or even year to year basis despite our mutual interest in pint drinking, poetry writing and the theatre. For many years this lack of personal contact was accounted for by a mere matter of geography; he lived in Kerry and I was—as I thought then, before happy chance ruled otherwise—permanently domiciled in Dublin, and the twain met only fitfully and infrequently. He might well have been residing in the Hindu Kush for all I knew of Kerry at that time and for many years prior to that. I had vague idyllic visions *a la* J. M. Synge whenever I thought of John B. scribbling dementedly away on the edge of the wild lonely Atlantic, writing his themes of sorrowful lost fierce people with their primitive passions and strange tongue tearing the flesh from each other with words. God knows what *he* thought of *me*, if he ever wasted time indulging in that unprofitable pursuit; some queer bloke in a wheelchair, maybe, up there in the concrete Nirvana of our unlovely capital city, spewing forth infantile verse and trying to knock down the walls of his own tawdry little Jericho with much noise and fury, signifying nothing very much. Later, when we did finally meet, I daresay the reality was slightly different for both of us, as reality has a habit of being, but meet we did, roaring out affectionate profanities to each other across the floor of his little pub in the handsome town of Listowel, as if we had known each other all our mortal days, though of course it was only to disguise the shyness and initial awkwardness the occasion held for us both. He said wise unflattering blustery things about my work and I said likewise about his and all in all hit it off rather well, without learning very much about each other, much like people everywhere.

Even then he had become something of a local legend and was fast becoming a national one, which of course aroused an instinctive and basically hostile curiosity in me, as I thought then, in my innocence, that most legends were largely self-made, especially literary ones. Once one has been made into or otherwise become a legend, at whatever level, it is damnably difficult to start behaving in any other way except as someone singled out by the gods—or demons—and raised above the common dust. The idea appeals to the vanity that is in all of us and is therefore surely not to be overly condemned or deplored or especially remarked upon, unless it gets out of hand and beyond the bounds of decency, so to speak, as of course it does only too often. So because he was already a legend and I was only a puny whisper in some kind persons' ear, I was more than ready to act the upstart peacock with him, this strong lyrical new messianic voice emanating out of the Kerry mountains, likewise so intimidating in their arrogant splendour and rugged individualism.

It was not like that at all, of course, for after that first tentatively defensive meeting, once I had put aside my narrow trite suspicions and received mythologies of "literary" people, I found myself being charmed out of my remaining wits by the warmth and humour and questing understanding of the man. I had both read and, later to my joy, seen *Sive*, that weirdly moving other-worldly play of bartered innocence and implacable tradition and superstition, and the impression it made upon me remains vividly in my mind today. Its theme was traditional, as earthy and poetic as any in Synge, but it appeared at a time of theatrical stagnation in Ireland, when the staple diet was still O'Casey and the name of The Abbey Theatre had become a dry dusty sound in many a throat, rather like a death-rattle that refused to stop and went interminably on and on until it lost all meaning. The literary scene in Dublin at that time was stiflingly claustrophobic, almost incestuous in its desperate camaraderie with a handful of gifted and talented men huddled together for warmth and inspiration against a largely indifferent and apathetic public that seemed to thrive in its collective set of government-approved blinkers; if there had been anything in existence remotely resembling a Free Welfare Service white canes would surely have been the first items to be handed out, an analogy not at all as far-fetched as it might seem. The valiant handful did trojan work, but Dublin was like a cell that was fast turning cancerous, with too much inbreeding enfeebling its finest efforts, one or two brilliant comets trailing innumerable insubstantial meteorites in their wake headed unalterably for the black densities of extinction. Into this enclosed arid wilderness *Sive* roared like a strange savage incantation, a raw wind from the broader wilder spaces of the land with its terrible immemorial message of love sold for silver pence, the casual betrayal of principle to the blind dictates of custom. *Sive* had arrived and we were all to be the better for it for the next decade or two.

Since honesty is the true basis of any friendship worth its salt, I will risk John B.'s wrath by confessing, to my shame, that until I was presented with *The Street & Other Poems*, I did not know that he wrote poetry *per se*, one at a time, line after line, stanza upon stanza, like any other member of that mad "sky-blue trade", and did not merely write poetry in the form of drama and meant exclusively for the stage. Well, it is never too late to make pleasant discoveries and I know better now. It is a sin of omission that weighs heavily on me, something due entirely to ignorance and not to any crass refusal to read his poetry out of mindless pique, that awful incurable disease called professional jealousy one hears so much about and which, to my horror, I have come into contact with once or twice in the course of my own working day. Yet the densest ignorance can be pierced and lightened, and I am not too dismayed by my own, since one would have to be as much under the earth as makes no matter not to realise that in his plays John B. Keane speaks as much with the voice of a poet as he writes with the hand of a craftsman; what, after all, is *Sive* if not one long dramatic poem, a Homeric ode set to music, so to speak, moving at its own deliberate and at times majestic pace towards final despair and tragedy? *Sharon's Grave* too, and some of the later plays, are richly poetic both in content and vision, with the same imperturbable leaning towards tragedy almost Greek in intensity as well as structure; one could think of the author in the guise of poet as playwright rather than the other way around, speaking with as intimate and singular a voice as in the volume of poems proper. His poetry loses nothing in being translated, as it were, for the stage, except the voice behind it is given more scope, different intonations and a wider range of expression.

Comparisons are, by and large, not just odious and unfair, since they can inflict more pain than any passing pleasure they bestow, but they can also be wildly irrelevant and abysmally abused, stuck into a review when the reviewer runs out of ideas, like raisins stuck into a plain cake to give it a bit of colour. Yet most things in life *are* derivative, whether we acknowledge that fact or not, and poetry is no lordly exception. There is no disgrace, surely, in echoing at least now and then the voice of our betters, those who went before us with the sign of faith? So I do not feel I am being particularly odious when I say that, in reading some of the poems in *The Street*, I catch faint but distinct echoes of Francis Ledwidge, albeit transposed from Meath to the wilder stretches of Kerry and spoken in a more rapid bustling tone; there is the same reflective texture to the words, the same intimate knowledge of landscape and nearness to earth, the joy and surprise in little things of field and hedge, river and tree, sky and wood. It would be an insult—and a terrible cliche into the bargain—to describe Keane's poetry as being possessed of "a rustic charm" and cosily leave it at that. Certainly it does have such a charm, rustic, rural, pastoral, whatever one wishes to choose from, as indeed how could it fail not to, written not only in but *out* of Kerry, under its fascinating ever-changing skies and enfolded by its brooding centurions of mountains and the sea that is never silent? But people are basically his main concern—I suppose this is where the playwright comes in, shrewd of eye and objective of motive—and he knows his people at least as well as he knows his fields and rivers and local configurations of land. There are the usual wry grotesqueries of country life clothed in the same deceptively simple garments; much whimsy about bachelor life and farm inheritance, breach of promise and udder-pulling, religious eccentricities and comic observations of widowed ladies no longer in their prime lusting none too secretly after healthy carefree young stallions flashing past on their stout bicycles or tractors. There is all this, the usual cast of characters presented for our amusement and titillation, yet much more, sad unwanted little insights into the things that people do to one another in the name of whatever emotion or idea that happens to be convenient at the time, sudden singular connections and affinities that are there one moment and gone the next, caught and pinned down to the page like butterflies but far from dead and breathing life still. His love poems are short, wistful and laconic, pruned of irritating detail, concise, condensed in their feeling and response. He recalls his father in a rueful loving way, makes clear his distrust and basic distaste of cities and the pity he feels for the people caught up in their myriad dens and mazes. His eye may be keen, even jaundiced at times, but it is never unkind, and if the canvas he uses is small it is alive with meticulously observed quirks and peculiarities of both people and places, things we can all see if we take the trouble but which only the poet can set down and bring to life again in the terrifying desolation and emptiness of a page of paper.

Having now had the pleasure of sampling his poetry as such for the first time, I now look forward to sampling the first pint John B. will ever have pulled for me, and I am confident it is something to which he will bring the same high degree of delicacy, diligence and robust craftsmanship. I doubt if at this advanced, not to say senile stage of our incarnation we will ever become "bosom pals", whatever that peculiarly inane euphemism might mean, for I believe we both share a distrust of "literary" friendships, having seen what damage such associations can cause and the multitude of falsehoods they can breed. Which is one of the reasons why some of my friends think I have latterly joined a Trappist monastery. But if our paths do tend to cross more often than heretofore, I hope we will remember to be friends first and brother bards second and thus lessen the frequency of mayhem. May his pen never flag or his typewriter give up the ghost. I am not at all worried about his Muse.

John B.'s Women

Phyllis Ryan

Long before the term "Women's Lib" became the catch-cry for female frustrations ranging from lesbianism to job inequalities, John B. Keane was writing plays featuring tough women with rebellious tendencies.

It is interesting to observe from his early plays onwards the development in his ladies; to follow the thought processes that make them unconventional despite the straitened, often barren conditions of their lives and marital circumstances. Just as that great play *The Field* is dominated by the awesome figure of The Bull McCabe, (one of the most famous male characters in Irish writing today and superbly created by Ray McAnally on the stage), so John B.'s line of strong-minded, liberated women exploded into the mammy of them all, the unforgettable Maggie Polpin, in perhaps his most popular play to date, *Big Maggie*.

Sive burst on the public first in 1959, presented by the Listowel Players and winning prizes and praise up and down the country until it seemed as though people were talking about nothing else. James N.

Healy had a great success with his production of the play in Cork and toured it afterwards to crowded houses and critical acclaim. There was controversy at the time about the failure of The Abbey Theatre to produce this phenomenally successful play. It was of no consequence as far as Keane and *Sive* were concerned. The play sailed blithely on, year after year, produced by groups in every part of Ireland and winning many awards in Drama Festivals. (I don't know who is doing it this year, but there will be a *Sive* somewhere, you can bet on that).

But although the two tinkers with their sinister song and chilling presence captured the imagination of critics and audiences alike and although the waif-like figure of Sive, pathetic in her ill-starred youth, draws tears from many, it is the character of Mena that compels our interest and controls our memory of the play. Thinking of *Sive*, one thinks first of Mena, the hard, unsympathetic wife who would condemn the hapless love-child to a life of misery with a rich, repulsive old man. Strange that such a character should be favoured despite the sweetness and youth of the tragic title-role! Strange that J. B. Keane's hard, unyielding women should command respect rather than dislike and understanding rather than total rejection. There is, of course, a reason and not only the obvious one—that John B. has had some marvellous actresses in his key roles. Who could forget the radiant Nora Relihan in *Sive*, or Anna Manahan as the ex-prostitute wife in *The Highest House on the Mountain*? The unique blend of comic and dramatic talent displayed by Maureen

Toal in *The Change in Mame Fadden*, and *The Good Thing* will not easily fade from memory, nor will the impact of any of the first Maggie Polpins. (There were five actresses of repute in Gemini's early production of *Big Maggie* and as I wish to stay alive in '79, I am not about to divulge my own favourite! There are limits to courage in all areas of life, and I am no Maggie Polpin). I cannot dismiss people lightly from my life, nor can I diminish them with Big Maggie's explanation for all her ruthless deeds, "'Tis for your good I am."

All that brings me back to the reason why John B. Keane's anti-heroines, such as Maggie and Mena, are not regarded by audiences as heartless villains. On the contrary, there is a certain sense of identification, if the parts are particularly well explored and the writer's insight into the roles achieved. The author has not created one-dimensional wicked-witch puppets. He has written about human beings who have survived in situations involving hard work, no play, and nothing much in the way of marital satisfaction. The meaning of the word love has been driven from their understanding by years of hard usage, as in the case of Maggie Polpin. The same barren hopelessness is evident in Mena's existence, driving her to bitter words and false assessments which end in tragedy for the whole family. But these women are not unfeeling monsters, obsessed with self-interest: Mena genuinely believed that "a good match" meant marrying money, and that Sive, being illegitimate, was fortunate to meet a doting old man willing to pay for his lust. Maggie Polpin always thought of the good of her children, but things had to be done her way. And they *were* done her way. At the end of the play, left alone, at loggerheads with her sons and daughters and most of the neighbourhood, she does not weaken. She refuses to take the easy way out and marry Byrne, her old admirer. Dismissing him, she starts making plans to carry on alone. "Life goes on," says Maggie, "and I have a business to run."

Of course it is inevitable that one should dwell on this larger-than-life but all too recognisable character, Big Maggie Polpin. No play I can remember in a life spent in theatre made such a powerful impact on the Irish playgoer. In terms of business, any previous records were broken all over the country. In terms of emotive response from audiences, it seemed they could not get enough of this play, and large numbers of people from every walk of life went four or five times to see it. There was, it appeared, a "Maggie Polpin" in every household. Gemini Productions, fortunate enough to be the first producers, found themselves involved in a play that was to make theatrical history. However, many years before *Big Maggie* was even a gleam in John B.'s eye, he was laying the foundations for a succession of sensational female roles, following *Sive* with a much-acclaimed drama called *The Highest House on the Mountain*. John had written it specially for the Dublin Theatre Festival of that year, and the cast contained such players as Martin Dempsey, Pat Nolan, Anna Manahan, Gerry Sullivan and one Jacqueline Ryan, then a schoolgirl and more reminiscent of Ondine than a healthy, rosy-cheeked country

Ray McAnally as 'The Bull' McCabe in 'The Field'

Publisher, Author and friend

lass. The play was a great success and caused an agreeable amount of shock to people whose minds were closed to the realities of life. One eminent critic compared Keane to Tennessee Williams, as both were writers who dealt poetically and fearlessly with love and sex. It was early days for that sort of thing!

The character of the ex-prostitute, desperately hoping to hide the secret of her past from her unsuspecting husband and trying to fend off the lustful advances of her widowed father-in-law was a foretaste of how different John B.'s women were likely to be! And Maimie, the publican's wife in *The Field* disgusted with her husband's lack of hygiene and intellect, flirts hungrily with any man who looks sideways at her and does more than flirt when the opportunity arises. This is her only form of protest against an unbearable existence. She is not naturally a "flier", but neither is she a model of resignation. And so, each successive script brought a new insight into the plight of women trapped by the conventions of rural society in a life bereft of colour or meaning. The growing resistance of Keane's women to slavery in the home or on the farm in a male-dominated society began to take positive shape.

In looking through the plays, and it would take more time and space than is now at my disposal to do justice to any one of them, let alone the many ultra-real people who stride through their pages, I realise more and more how Keane's key women are trapped by their common life factors. Tradition, snobbery, greed and poverty, all implacable enemies of the love and warmth these women desired, hardened their attitudes and warped their basic tenderness. Many of the failures and virtues of the traditional system of arranging marriages are illustrated by the presence in the plays of "The Matchmaker" figure—wily, diplomatic and colourful. If this familiar and often richly comic figure is absent, the matches are made by the families directly and in either case daughters are sold like cattle to the highest bidder.

We also begin to discover that the "girls" as opposed to the "women" in Keane's plays suffer from the strength of their senior counterparts, and therefore, as in most works for the theatre the juvenile parts are not the most showy or the most sought after by actors and actresses. Those necessary younger women, who are mainly re-actors to the dominant female characters, impinge on the consciousness much in the same way that victims, dead by accident or murder, gain importance merely as fodder for the over-powering forces that cause their demise. The dead youth is forgotten while one dwells on the fearsome power of the lightning that burnt out his life. The drunken driver lives on in newsprint and vengeful musing long after we have forgotten who was crushed beneath his wheels. The murderer, known or un-detected, takes up the most of our imagining. It is the strong who command our attention, regardless of deed or motive and it is this inherent ability to change the course of events against all odds that fashions Keane's maturer women into powerful symbols of feminist activity. And this many years ahead of the women's equality movement prevailing so universally today. *Sharon's Grave* is a poetic and beautiful play in which the extremes of good and evil are embodied in human personalities. This play, although based upon folklore, is no fairy-tale. It is an elemental expression of the forces of innocence and bestiality buried in the human soul. These forces are brought into fierce conflict when Dinsey, the veritable spawn of evil, confronts the young heroine in a scene so macabre that the audience, like the girl, are hypnotised and held captive by its chilling content. Dinsey, crippled in mind and body, uses his brother's strong limbs to carry him to the brink of his own destruction. But the girl survives the torrent of lust and greed loosed by Dinsey in that final dark encounter. Her only weapons are faith and love, qualities which have been known to move mountains and mow down armies of opposition. In this lovely play the younger characters, simple folk shaped by the wild beauty of their surrounding home-land, hold the winning cards.

This is rare enough in Keane's work for theatre. Certainly, most of his key parts for women are written for the more mature members of the gentler sex. Of course, there is more dramatic substance in the person who has lived long enough to look back as well as forward than there is in the adolescent on the threshold of life. Much has been written about teenagers in the last few years. Novels, songs, plays and poems have extolled their virtues, deplored their addictions, understood them, analysed their moods, and blamed their parents and mentors for most of their symptoms. A great deal of money has been made for a great many people form the cult of the young in this generation. But you will search in vain for signs of the "Teenage Cult" in any of John B. Keane's writings. He digs in well-tilled soil for a richer harvest. His orchards have been many years attaining their golden fruits. Keane's women have weathered the seasons, the best and the worst and we who listen in the stalls are often humbled by their endurance and survival.

"Were there but world enough and time" for all Keane's women to be analysed, understood, loved, hated, it would be a rewarding exercise for any student of drama. Many of the plays and characters must be left out of this article, and no attempt has been made to do an 'in depth" analysis of any one of them. But particular mention must be made of J. B. Keane's most recent play, *The Good Thing*. Here you have three sisters re-united at the wedding of a mutual friend. Two of the sisters have married well, but unhappily. The third, Maudie, has married a poor man doing what her snobbish sisters refer to as menial work and is as happy with her lot as most of us would wish to be. Maudie is plump, vivacious and sexy. She has weathered years of marriage and motherhood, constantly "pulling the divil by the tail", bolstered against the bad times by natural good humour. The wealthy, neglected wives in this play display traits which qualify them for the roles of the ugly sisters against Maudie's lovable Cinderella. Smart clothes and hair-do's do not always things of beauty make! When the embittered pair decide to give their husbands a taste of their own medicine, all hell breaks loose. Eve, the younger sister, sick of her husband's womanising, goes on the town herself and after a few drinks and a quick "bedding" with a total stranger, confronts her husband with a sense of triumphant liberation. Her older sister succumbs to the charms of an "old flame" and pays her husband for years of neglect by cuckolding him. The same night, Maudie's husband Mickie, beats her up in a fit of drunken jealousy. This enrages Maudie's sisters so much that they try to persuade her to leave him, and enjoy some of the fleshpots that have not been too evident in her impoverished existence.

But here again one glimpses the "moral" in the story, and discovers who is really the stronger. In a totally unexpected turn-about, we find that the strength lies not in the two "liberated" sisters, who now feel they have their men by the short hairs, but in the simple, undemanding Maudie, contented, home-loving, and able to forgive her erring man. *The Good Thing* was received with shock and unbelief when it was first seen in the country. The general reaction was that "this kind of thing couldn't happen here" . . . "I mean, a man might stray now and then, sure isn't it his nature? But for his wife to do the same . . ." . . . 'Oh no, John B. Keane has overstepped himself this time . . . " However, a surprising number of people managed to identify with all the women in the play, and the box-office didn't suffer.

In all John B.'s women, even the ones who seem larger than life in ferocity and domination, there is a richly comic element which leavens the acid in their souls. This endears them to audiences even when their deeds merit public rejection. Maggie, Maudie, Maimie, and even Mena have the power from the playwright to bring tears of laughter as well as the other kind. Even in that tragic play, *The Year of the Hiker*, where an ailing old man, wishing to return home to die, encounters savage opposition from a woman who once loved him and has nurtured resentment and revenge in her bosom for over twenty years, there are moments when the playwright's humour shines in one or other of the characters, so that all is not unrelieved gloom.

But perhaps John B.'s strangest woman character is the exception that proves the rule, as she is neither forceful nor aggressive, nor is there light in her darkness. In *The Change in Mame Fadden*, the writer explores the difficult time in a woman's life when she reaches the menopause. Mame Fadden is a woman who has never known real tenderness or honest passion. Her husband is pompous and boring, and like many sensitive beings Mame has come to accept her soulless existence, running her house and bringing up her children with decorum; staying quietly in the background and suppressing all natural urges until they ceased to cause pain. Until the advent of the menopause. Then her erratic behaviour begins to disturb her husband and family and cause uneasy ripples in their smooth life-styles. Mame takes to walking along the quayside late at night, and to shouting hysterically into the secluded avenue from the window of her room. All the pain of loss rises to the surface, as the consciousness of the barren past assails her, and the knowledge that there is no "magic casement" opening up in her vision of the future. Youth is finally dead. In her case it was battered to death early by the boorish insensitivity of her husband; his selfish ambitions which were not for *her* sharing; and the heartless indifference of her children.

Fearing that Mame's "nightwalking", plus her public outbursts and generally uncontrolled behaviour may make the neighbours murmur and deprive the family of social climbing on a grander scale, Mame's family and in-laws try to persuade her to go into a nursing home. Eventually they decide to commit her, with the help of a "friendly" physician. Mame Fadden is far from insanity, but she is only too aware that she cannot find the answer to her own inner tumult. She finds distraction in talks with lonely fellow-wanderers on the quays; she hears stories of broken lives and broken marriages, and she pleads, literally for her life, for help from her husband. Mame Fadden has no place to go. She knows the years have caught up with her, and she cannot regain the joyous image of her belief in what life should hold. The riches imbued in a truly loving relationship are lost to her forever. She must face the future never knowing the meaning of passion, never knowing real happiness, never giving birth to dreams more relevant to her than flesh and blood realities. As an alcoholic craves liquor, Mame craves understanding and solace. But realising that she cannot help herself through her present depressions, and terrified by the nightmares conjured up by the word "Hospital", she is driven to take the only way out that seems likely to ease all trouble.

Most compassionately, John B. Keane is able to see through the darkness in the "quiet ones" and find out the delicate springs that trigger off many aspects of a woman's behaviour. His understanding of women is incredible, when one comes to think of how few male authors have written parts for actresses with the same subtlety and insight as they have for actors. A very famous actress once said to me, on seeing her fifth Keane play in my company: "Thank God at least *one* man cares enough about women to do a bit of research on the subject, and thank God he writes leading roles for women that you can really get your teeth into!" Without John B. Keane's women, theatre would be a poorer place for those of us who wear the skirts. In John B.'s plays, we can sometimes wear the pants, and the shirts, and still retain our status as wives, mothers, lovers, and friends of . . . MEN.

Fear an Mhisnigh

Caoimhín Ó Marcaigh

Ní chuireann tú aithne cheart ar dhuine, a deir an seanfhocal go dtagann an duine sin chun cónaithe leat. Ní bhíonn aithne agat ar údar, a deir an foilsitheoir, go dtí go ndéanann tú leabhar i gcomhar leis.

Ní raibh aithne agam ar John B. Keane go dtí gur scríobh sé *Dan Pheaidí Aindí*. Ó, d'ith mé dinnéir ina chomhluadar, chuala mé é ag cur draíochta ar chomhluadair le bhriathra meala is beagáinín den aigéad tríothu. Léigh mé a chuid leabhar. Chonaic mé a chuid drámaí. Ní hionann san agus aithne a chur ar dhuine.

Nuair a bhí *Dan Pheaidí Aindí* á ullmhú do na clódóirí bhínn go minic i dteagmháil leis an údar faoi rudaí beaga. Ba í an umhlaíocht an tréith ba shuntasaí san údar sna comhráití sin, é fíorbhuíoch den té a chuirfeadh laige sa téacs ar a shúile dó nó a dhéanfadh moladh faoi seo nó faoi siúd. Ní hionann sin is a rá go n-áiteofá rud ar bith air nach mbeadh sé sásta leis. Ba léir freisin an t-omós a bhí aige don teanga seo nár scríobh sé mórán inti roimhe seo. Bhí níos mó ná ómós i gceist. Bhraith mé go rabhas ag caint le tiománaí a raibh gluaisteán nua faoi, a bhí ar bís chun é a thástáil.

Ghlaoigh mé ar John B. maidin amháin. Rith sé liom go mbeadh sliocht áirithe ina scríbhinn níos éifeachtaí dá n-aistreofaí é amach go deireadh an leabhair. Chuir mé scairt air chun an méid sin a chur ina chead.

"Cén sliocht é?" ar seisean.

Léas amach dó ar an bhfón an chéad abairt den sliocht. Lean seisean ar aghaidh leis an gcuid eile den phíosa a bhí i gceist, focal ar fhocal. An caolsheans go raibh an láimhscríbhinn lena uillinn nuair a ghlac sé an glaoch teileafóin; agus fiú dá mbeadh, ní bhfaigheadh sé teacht ar an sliocht úd chomh gasta sin. Caithfidh go raibh an t-iomlán fós ina cheann.

An chéad uair eile a bheas muid ag obair le chéile triallfad an rud chéanna arís air. Ní mór dom mo theoraic a thástáil. Tá sórt tuairime agam go gcoinníonn John B. a shaothar reatha ar ribín ríomhaireachta na hintinne go dtí go dtéann an leabhar sin i gcló.

Táim go mór faoi chomaoin ag John B. faoin leabhar úd *Dan Pheaidí Aindí*. Thug sé an-mhisneach dom. Seo fear ildánach a thuill cáil dó féin i dteanga amháin a bhí sásta anois tabhairt faoi leabhar cruthaitheach i dteanga eile. Is cuma cé chomh maith is a bhí a chuid Gaeilge ní raibh an mhuinín, an taithí, an stór focal, an cora cainte Cathánach aige faoi mar a bhí i mBéarla. Ní fhéadfadh a bheith. Mar sin féin bhí an misneach aige, misneach lena chlú a chur i bhfiontar. Mhínigh sé dom ar ball gur thóg sé a chúig oiread ama air *Dan Pheaidí Aindí* a scríobh agus a chaithfeadh sé le leabhar i mBéarla. Agus bhí imní air i rith an ama nach mbeadh an saothar inghlactha i ndeireadh báire. Ar ndóigh, ní raibh aon dealramh leis an imní. Thuill a leabhar, in éineacht le leabhar Bhreandáin Uí Eithir, *Willie the Plain Pint agus an Pápa*, thuilleadar eatarthu *Books Ireland* Award sa bhliain 1978, an chéad uair a raibh leabhar Gaeilge i measc na mbuathóirí.

Gaeilge a labhair John B. i gcónaí liomsa agus bhí ionadh, agus éad, riamh orm go raibh Gaeilge chomh blasta ag duine nach ndearna é a chleachtadh rómhinic le blianta beaga anuas. Níos measa ná sin, bhí sé amuigh ar John go raibh sé ina namhaid *cláraithe* ag an nGaeilge ón uair a thug sé tacaíocht d'eagraíocht a bhí ann chun deireadh a chur le Gaeilge éigeantach, má bhí sé ann ar chor ar bith. Bhí John B. ar an mbeagán san eagraíocht úd a thug tacaíocht di de bharr grá, seachas fuath, don teanga. Tá an méid sin cruthaithe anois aige, agus creidim go gcruthóidh sé é arís is arís eile amach anseo. Tá an dara leabhar á scríobh aige i nGaeilge agus níl amhras orm ach go n-éireoidh leis faoi mar a d'éirigh le *Dan Pheaidí Aindí.*

Bíonn amhras ar leabhardhíoltóirí faoi leabhair i nGaeilge go minic. Ní thógaim orthu é. Ní fheiceann siad an t-uafás díobh agus an uair a fheiceann ní féidir a mheas roimhré cén éileamh a bheadh orthu. Go leor de na leabhair úd chuirfidís le clú an tsiopa ach ní chuirfidís mórán lena theacht isteach. Is ar an ábhar sin a chreidim go gcuireann John B. comaoin ar fhoilsitheoireacht na Gaeilge i gcoitinne nuair a scríobhann sé leabhar dúinn i nGaeilge.

Aithníonn siopadóirí an t-ainm láithreach. Seo é an té a dtig leis an fhoilsitheoir deich míle cóip dá leabhair a dhíol leo sula mbíonn aon chuid ach an clúdach ar fáil. Sea, rachaidh leabhardíoltóirí sa tseans le John B. i nGaeilge agus, os rud é gur éirigh go maith lena chéad leabhar Gaeilge is fearr an tseans atá ann go nglacfaidh siad le leabhair Gaeilge le húdair eile.

Ní thig linn ach aon chaighdeán amháin feabhais a bheith againn sa tír. Is cuma a gceapaimid go bhfuil sé cothrom nó nach gceapann, táimid in iomaíocht in áit an mhargaidh le leabhair i mBéarla. Is inti a shlánófar foilsitheoireacht na Gaeilge. Agus déanfaimid é le cabhair údair ar nós John B. Keane.

Is aoibhinn le muintir na hÉireann stíl grinn John B. I gcás Dan Pheaidí Aindí Uí Shúilleabháin bíonn an léitheoir ag gáire faoi eachtraí an chleamhnasaí ach ní dhéanann an t-údar fonóid faoi Dan riamh. Tá meas an údair ar ábhair an ghrinn ríshoiléir. Idir shúgradh agus dáiríre atá sé. Más greannmhar leis imeachtaí Dan mar úinéir halla rince is mar fhear déanta cleamhnas briseann an dáiríreacht tríd an greann ar uaire.

Bhí daoine ann, más fíor, a d'ionsaigh Dan faoi go ndearna sé airgead as cleamhnais a dhéanamh. I bpíosa atá chomh maith le haon rud atá scríofa aige i mBéarla déanann John B. achoimre ar shaol agus ar shaothar a sheancharad. Ní haon plámás ná déanamh gaisce é. Níl ann ach blúirín beag staire:

'Bhí an-chuid de chustaiméirí Dan sna daichidí agus san caogaidí. Bhí neirbhís nó easpa misnigh ar a lán acu ceal taithí ar chuideachta daoine. Chuadar níos domhaine fós sa duibheagán agus san éadóchas toisc gan bheith ábalta meascadh lena gcomharsana. Chríochnaíodar, ar deireadh, ina n-oileáin—deighilte amach ón saol a bhí timpeall orthu—agus fágadh iad gan dóchas, gan áit le dul, gan suim ar bith san am a bhí le teacht. Théadh Dan i dtreo na ndaoine seo uaidh féin, gan cuireadh. Chonaic sé an iomarca dá leithéidí "á seoladh siar to Cill Áirne". Ní raibh aon chlinicí sna bailte an uair sin, ná ní raibh aon bhanaltraí síceolaíochta ag gabháil timpeall na dúichí faoi mar atá anois. Mar sin bhí Tigh na nGealt i gCill Áirne lán suas de dhaoine dá sórt. Níor cheart go gcuirtí cuid acu isteach ann riamh, ach ní raibh aon dul as ag lucht leighis an tráth sin.'

B'shin mar a bhí ag muintir Ladhair a Chrompáin sna daicheadaí. Ba é sin dúthaigh Shaidhbh agus muintir Glavin freisin. Ó shin i leith thaistil John B. níos faide i gcéin ina chuid saothair. Ach is soiléir go mbeidh air filleadh arís is arís eile ar an gceantar sin. D'fhág sé scór dráma agus leabhar ann.

The Art and Craft of John B. Keane

ROBERT HOGAN

OF COURSE, one's first inclination is to write of John B. Keane simply as a person. It would be easy enough, Lord knows, to launch into a string of anecdotes that illustrated his warmth and kindness, his humour and wit, and the ease and charm and grace that have rarely deserted him, and that have always been a brake against mere eccentricity.

Eccentricity is often taken for character, and most of us probably tend to reduce a really rare and complex character to a simple Jonsonian humour. It is easier, and perhaps even more fun, to see a Bernard Shaw simply as a bearded Pierrot, or a Chesterton simply as a Christian Falstaff. And so there is this tendency to make John B. into a semi-cultured culchie or a rube who writes. And that makes it easy to explain away the successes of his writing by his personality, and, conversely, to lay the failures to his having remained so defiantly a Kerryman.

As there have been enough successes for John B. to be known all over the country, such an attitude may be satisfying enough to the *amour propre* of the Kingdom. Still, it does give the academics or the Dublin literati the effective rejoinder that being the Kerryman-playwright means being out of the main current of the time, and not being influenced by the best of what is happening in the intellectual world, or the literary world, or even—if anything ever does happen there—the theatrical world.

There is some truth, both good and bad, in this point of view, for much that John B. writes is suffused by his personality—the essays and epistolary novelettes probably more than the plays. I have heard it said, often enough for it to become a cliche, that his personality is what carries his stuff through, and makes it work, at least enough for a few laughs, and despite the lack of artistry and craftsmanship. A fair rejoinder, however, would be that many of the finest of modern writers have been ones like Dickens, like Mark Twain, like Wilde and Shaw, like Dylan Thomas, like O'Casey and Brendan Behan, whose personality permeates their work and enriches it immensely more than a lot of psychically anonymous masterpieces that one could easily enough mention.

No, that kind of individuality, if one is lucky enough to have it, is a godsend and one of the strongest weapons in a writer's armoury. Probably it is not enough by itself to make a work of art; and, as much as I dote on them, I would have to admit that there are a lot of dull patches even in Dickens and Mark Twain, patches where they try to make it simply on personality.

So it is as an artist, then, that any writer is going to be remembered—not as a local character, or a genial publican, or even as a butter salesman, but simply as an artist. An artist, I take it, has something to say, and has the craft to say it with power and passion, with humour and with heart. A hack, I take it, has not much to say, but finds his own little garden of romance, adventure, sex, espionage, religion or whatever, and assiduously tills it ever after. His name does not have to be Earl Stanley Gardner or Dennis Wheatley; it can be P. G. Wodehouse or Georgette Heyer or even Anthony Trollope, delightful hacks, and one wishes they had written even more books. Maurice Walsh also, whether he was writing about Scotland or Ireland, was such a delightful and brilliant hack that one re-reads him as one re-reads John Buchan or Captain Marryat, and as one does not re-read Hemingway who had considerably more pretensions to artistry.

John B., I think, has some very legitimate claims to artistry. For one thing, the worlds of Wodehouse or Heyer or Trollope or Maurice Walsh are static, unchanging. They are never-never lands, Cloud-Cuckoo lands, Grecian Urn lands; and we like to go back to them because we know they are unchanging. We know that it will not rain there, that the girls will always be fair and bright, that simple courage and an honest heart will finally win out over the rotters and cads. Above all, we know that the moral visions are as solid and immutable and unchanging as the Rock of Gibraltar.

And, of course, these superb hacks have the craft to hypnotise us into believing, momentarily, that their manikins have a too, too solid flesh that will never melt, and an ethic so, so solid that the gates of hell shall never prevail against it. And perhaps that really is a good thing. Certainly it has seemed a good thing when I have put down some lovely hack book and sallied out, D'Artagnan in a trench coat—well, Cyrano anyway—to cope with what seems, momentarily a Walt Disney world.

The real world that the real person copes with, and that the real artist writes about, is not very solid. Fifty years ago, or a hundred, or two hundred, there were thousands of enclaves all over the world that seemed utterly fixed, established, permanent; and whose ethic was utterly fixed, established, permanent. I say "seemed" because the permanence was not really real; and it only took a Famine or a Land War or a Civil War to make ethics just about as stable as a plateful of quivering jelly.

Perhaps Kerry was such an enclave longer than many places, and so could pride itself on being more moral than the rest of the world, when in reality it was only more isolated. But all that has changed, changed utterly, thanks to motor cars and foreign investment and Vatican II and the E.E.C. and Elvis movies and even Telefís Éireann. So as the immense cloud of homogeneity blankets more and more of the world, the old verities get swamped by the new neuroses. The cowboy heroes now wear black hats, and there's no way anymore to tell the good guys from the bad.

The artist in such a changing world either has to keep changing what he talks about, or he has to talk about the world of the past or the world of Cloud-Cuckoo land. A very fine artist like Michael Molloy, partly because he is older than John B., opts to talk about the past; obviously someone needs to, for that is one way of not entirely losing our grip on the present. John B., in his first three folk plays, was really talking about the past also. In *Sive*, in *The Highest House on the Mountain*, and in *Sharon's Grave*, a past Ireland was remembered with terrific impact. It was an Ireland that dozens of other writers had remembered or recreated or celebrated, but I think that those three plays made their special impact partly because of the time in which they were written, but mainly because of their considerable artistry. *Sive*, for instance, is awfully close in subject and in theme and in characters to Louis D'Alton's *Lovers Meeting*, which was a pretty good play, sound, well-observed and craftsmanlike enough for the Abbey to revive it in the Queen's about 1960. Yet *Lovers Meeting* in 1960 did not have much of an impact, and John B.'s play, which came along at about the same time, did. A chief reason was the two tinkers in *Sive*. They and their song utterly lifted that play, and gave people a kind of shock of recognition. What was recognised was not any naturalistic fidelity, for the tinkers were basically theatre stuff, but their theatricality stood for the richness of a past that was still rememberable, and that they made memorable. The other two early plays, particularly *Sharon's Grave*, had the same kind of richness, and John B. could certainly have continued dishing up racial nostalgia. It is much to his credit as an artist that he did not, that he said new things.

John B.'s first decade of professional writing was the 1960s, and that decade in Ireland and in Kerry was one in which the pace of change accelerated immensely. There was a widening gap between the old and the new, and John B.'s new plays charted how the old attempted to accommodate itself to the new, or even to fight against it.

Many Young Men of Twenty, with its haunting title song, was, for all its fine comedy, a dirge and a lament. Like O'Casey's glum *The Bishop's Bonfire*, it showed that old ways had lost, and that a stream of emigrants was taking the mailboat to the modern world. *Hut 42* shows what happened when they got there, and how they mourned for what they had lost. There was nothing awfully new about the theme; a hundred songs have been written about the Irish emigrant and some powerful novels by Patrick MacGill. What is in the mind, however, of the patrons of hundreds of Irish bars in New York and Boston; what is assuredly in the mind of insane old men in the Bronx who make rousing speeches about contributing money to the IRA; and what is patently scrawled across the beaming and flushed face of every Yank as he gets off his Aer Lingus charter at Shannon, is the appalling certainty that nothing has changed. Cloud-Cuckoo Land is revisited. And that, for the most part, is what is in the mind of the characters in these plays.

But in the next plays, the old nostalgia begins to be dissipated by the new disaffection. The unpublished *No More in Dust* is also a lament, only this time the modern world is not in Camden Town but in Dublin. The Edna O'Brienish country girls in their seedy Leeson Street flat bemoan the past that their parents have pushed them out of. But in this instance the past is not entirely seen through green-coloured spectacles. The young countryman up from Kerry for the weekend deserts the girl who has fallen in love with him, and is something of a rat.

That fact probably confuses the statement of *No More in Dust* somewhat, and the confusion hovers over a much better play, *The Year of the Hiker.* The Hiker Lacey is something of a legendary figure, Ireland's past really, and when he comes home to his children, he is subdued and battered and rather catatonic. The children belong to the new Ireland, and the father is an awkward anachronism—dirty, stupid, repulsive and strange. But he is finally accepted with punishment, then resignation, then sympathy, and then some chilly affection. And why not? He will die soon anyway.

The theatre is a morally simple place, much more so than the streets outside. As the most gormless member of any audience, I keep wanting the Hiker to be eloquent, flamboyant, rich in spirit, and to flagellate his children for their shrivelled modern souls. Nostalgia, nostalgia. Cloud-Cuckoo land revisited, and John B.'s allegory here about the modern and the old is certainly right, but he should have made it a novel, for novel readers are more sophisticated and nastier people than playgoers. Or maybe he should have written it better.

A more successful play, but not as good a one, is *The Man from Clare.* It is more successful because the issues are simpler. Athletics had become a form of sublimation; it kept young men out of the pubs, kept their minds off sex or revolution or economic discontent, dissipated energy, kept them docile and tractable and childlike. In this play, the mentally adolescent hero becomes finally mentally adult; and the Ireland of the thirties and forties and fifties is seen as an adolescent that must grow up and live in the modern world. The problem was true enough, but narrower and simpler than the big problem in *The Year of the Hiker*.

John B.'s views are not really simple, and he has not written a progressively charted series of plays that show how the modern world must, and, indeed, should overwhelm the old. There is an ambivalence about his attitude toward the old values and the new that make him a perceptive man of his transitionary time, as well as an appropriate artist for it. For instance, *The Field* is one of his best plays, and it shows that the old anachronistic ways have so much vigour left in them that they defeat everything that the modern state and the modern church can throw against them. However, the defeat of the new is regarded with some mournfulness, with some sad sense of failure; and the Bull McCabe stands as much for an uncivilised and heartless parochialism as he does for a rich indomitability.

Big Maggie is a kind of companion play to *The Field* and the dominating mother is the female equivalent of the Bull McCabe; only this play shows her as a more anachronistic figure than he even, for, whether she admits it or not, she has lost everything that she has saved for.

And then there are his quite modern plays that no one would have predicted after seeing *Sive* in 1959. *The Change in Mame Fadden*, really for the first time in an Irish play, takes up the psychological problem of menopause. *The Good Thing* takes up the ferocious sexual problems, the frustration and the boredom and the disillusion, that so often set in after ten years of marriage. Sex has been discussed in Irish novels for the enormous psychological problem that it can be, much earlier and more frequently than it has been in plays. Plays are a public form of art, and the playgoer, even the hardened Broadway playgoer, still goes to a lot of plays as if he were a first communicant approaching the altar. There is a good deal to be said for this—and a good deal to be said against it. However, Pegeen Mike never even kisses Christy, and Jack Clitheroe only sings a sentimental song to Nora. Would that the relations of human beings in the modern world were no more traumatic.

It would have been impossible for the miasma that is often sexuality to have been discussed by an Irish playwright before the 1970s. I do not think that John B., in either *The Change in Mame Fadden* or *The Good Thing*, discusses them brilliantly, but there is an honesty, a candour, that could probably not have been there before the world changed.

And John B.'s other things? Myself, I do not think that they are awfully important, and the reason is craftsmanship. It used to be fashionable to say that D. H. Lawrence wrote only with "the hot blood's blindfold art," rather than with the canniness and judgment of Henry James or E. M. Forster or Virginia

Woolf. It is probably still fashionable to say that Eugene O'Neill had all the talents necessary to write great tragedy except the ability to write. Both opinions struck me as foolish, and so is the similar opinion that I have so often heard about Keane.

No one, though, writes so much and so often effectively simply out of luck or personality or pure and untutored talent. Conscious craft and overt judgment are necessary, and it would be simple enough to pick out scores of passages from Keane's plays or epistolary novelettes, and demonstrate how he gets such good effects. But that sort of analysis is for the classroom; here, it seems important only to suggest that John B. is probably a good deal more uneven than many less talented writers. There are a couple of short plays that friends should have restrained him from publishing; there are some of the *Letters of . . .* where the invention badly flags; and, finally, there are some of his very best things that need more brooding on, more honing and more polishing. For instance, his play, *The Good Thing*, is an eminently worthy attempt to grapple with a most significant subject. Yet one of the characters, the silent drunken husband, is a simple theatrical joke; yet the sexuality of one of the wives is more out of *Playboy* magazine than out of life; yet the texture of the dialogue is too rough—too many easy lines, theatrical lines, and trite lines which undercut the psychology and the importance of the whole business.

Everybody works to a different speed, and often the best things come in a flash. Noel Coward wrote *Private Lives* in four days, and Alan Ayckbourn wrote his whole triology, *The Norman Conquests*, in twelve. In both cases, I should say somewhat dryly, it certainly shows. And even Shakespeare who wrote so well and so facilely that everybody walks around with a headful of quotations from him, even Shakespeare who never blotted a line, should—according to rare Ben Johnson—have blotted a thousand.

But this perhaps is critic's talk, and I am mindful that Paul Vincent Carroll once said to me, "like all critics you can be a right bitch at times." (Of course, he did go on to say, "But I suppose God in his Wisdom made critics that way.")

Well, well, now that poor old John B. is entering his sixth decade, tottering into his dotage, losing the hair on the crown of his head, what may we—the hairy and vigorous young—expect from him? Some more *Letters of* . . ., or droll essays, the occasional story and poem, a play every year on some new ghastliness that the modern Irishman will encounter in his brave new world? That would be fine, of course; and it would do what John's work has always done in the past—that is, make all of us a little bit more tolerant of living with each other, a little warmer, a little better even. Yet what I would really like is the Big Play. Compared to Shaw, John B. (decayed as he is) is but a callow stripling still; and Shaw, when he was older than John, tried for the really big things, and wrote *Heartbreak House*, *Saint Joan* and *Back to Methuselah*. So try for the big thing, John, and take your time about it. After all, whether you make it or miss it, you'll pull the rest of us up a bit for trying.

All the best, a mhic.

Letter to an Authentic Genius

TONY BUTLER

DEAR JOHN,

The celebration of your fiftieth birthday gives Ireland an opportunity to salute one of its most brilliant writers. Be modest if you must but time and history will take no heed of your protests. It is no passing adulation which compels me to assert that you rank with Swift, Synge, O'Casey, Yeats, Behan and Leonard and you have achieved a greatness which is a noble addition to the treasury of our literature.

All that you are sings of Ireland and reflects in particular the laughter-sown, poetry-blossomed, beauty-decked earth of Kerry. In turn Ireland and Kerry have shaped and sculptured your talents, your skills and your personality. In a sense the great Atlantic waves have beached on your soul; your psyche has been thrown to the skies with the mountains and the heavy, weary clouds that plod the meadows of the sea have, at times, shrouded your vision with a dark awareness of the ultimate emotions.

The human fabric of your home town, Listowel, must be remembered for it is rich with traditions and an inspiring pattern of events. There the imagination cannot remain easy and the language of the streets and the countryside rinse the ear with echoes of the old Irish vernacular from which the modern English of Kerry has been distilled. Idioms, structures and lilt all stem from Gaelic and its rich past of poetry and creative vision; its memory of courts and kings and its suggestions of ancient and terrible religions. The inspirations it offers can be seen in the work of other Listowel writers such as Bryan McMahon, Brendan Kennelly, Micheál Ó hAodha, Maurice Walsh and George Fitzmaurice.

In the vicinity of Listowel also there is much that is curious and stimulating. On the coast of Astee, Jesse James, the great train robber, is claimed for the village and about four miles from your public house is the shooting lodge of Gunnsborough where the future looter of Khartoum, Lord Kitchener was born.

But Listowel has a special air. There's the gentle rambling of the Feale river and the tight streets wound around the church-centred square like thread on a bobbin. The square too must remind you that it was there Parnell asserted that no man has a right to fix the boundaries of a nation. You probably know as well that the people of Knocknagoshel made history that week by creating a slogan of monumental arrogance, "Arise Knocknagoshel and take your place amongst the Nations of the Earth".

I also suppose that you were influenced directly or indirectly by that great Listowel bookseller, Dan

Flavin, who corresponded with Axel Munthe and obtained for himself and his friends one of the first copies of James Joyce's *Ulysses*.

It was a great place to see the first day of your life on 21 July 1928 even though, as you wrote later, "Apart from my birth it was an uneventful year, free of plague, war and famine". You did a fine job with your autobiography *Self Portrait* which captures all of your fine character; your truths and your honesty. It has too that peculiar Irish quality of sacrificing the most sacred and serious moments for the divine consolation of laughter. And why not? Laughter, it can be said, is a form of prayer and you've helped many a sinner in your time.

Your autobiography gives the impression of a man who has a great capacity for contentment and peaceful living and it is easy to understand why you came home from England after some two years working as a scavenger, barman, labourer and furnace operator.

Admittedly it wasn't the noblest career in the world to which you came back and apart from making pile ointments for the aristocratic arse of Lord Doneraile life must have been dull at first but, thank God, you got back to Listowel. Your home town and marriage combined to unlock the vast creative power that the years stored up in the deeper recesses of your being. *Sive* was not the creation of the fourteen days you spent in writing; it was the many years of association with environment, history, traditions, friends, folkways and all else that gave it majestic being.

I've told you before that *Sive* must be numbered amongst the great plays of our time. You have, to be sure, produced enough to furnish several reputations with the material of enduring fame but *Sive* is your masterpiece, the proud gauntlet you've flung in the face of posterity. More, it is a work which reflects your talents and your vision in a special way. To know the play is to know all your creative powers. For that reason it repays study and it may be taken as the matrix of your developing genius.

The full story of how *Sive* came to splendid and triumphant realisation is told with heart-gripping tension in Gus Smith's *Festival Glory in Athlone*. Although the book tells the epic story of modern amateur drama in Ireland it is you and *Sive* which dominate the story. The blazing triumph of the play and its vivid success is fascinating but the narrative does a lot to illuminate the malicious arrogance which so often mars the relationship of The Abbey Theatre with some of our playwrights.

Their rejection of the play after a mere five weeks suggests it wasn't read with any seriousness. The fact that they failed to send you some form of critical evaluation is equally indicative of their aesthetic myopia.

No, it wasn't their first error of judgment that merits serious condemnation; it was their refusal to acknowledge later that they had kept a major play out of the repertoire of our National Theatre which merits the most contemptuous scorn. Is it not extraordinary and thickheaded that you, a major Irish playwright, should have hardly any place in the year to year productions of The Abbey Theatre?

It is not alone *Sive* which should have an honoured place in their repertoire but the rest of your plays merit production from time to time. The brutal and terrible horror of *Sharon's Grave*; the dramatic juggernaut of *The Field* and the ballad swing of *Many Young Men of Twenty* all merit recognition no less than other products of your inspired pen. When they can devote extravagant sums to the scrapings of the national dramatic latrines they could be expected to devote a little to the rich and unsullied protein of your plays. But that's something for another day.

Your radio play *Barbara Shearing* was an excellent start to your development as a playwright but there were all those plays—some say there were forty—on which you cut your literary teeth. *Sive* was no accident.

Gus Smith, as I mentioned, has traced the history of *Sive* from its first production by the Listowel Drama Group to their ultimate triumph with it at Athlone when they won the Esso cup, the supreme award of the All-Ireland Amateur Drama Festival. All in all, 1959 must have been a year you'll not forget.

I've heard that in moments of creation you nourish your imagination with pints of stout and hard-boiled eggs, with pig's pudding in reserve for the more difficult scenes. In spite of that knowledge one must ask what is the secret of the enduring appeal of *Sive*?

You have not, as of yet, attracted the full attention of some academics but Robert Hogan in *After the Irish Renaissance* gives your achievements the serious consideration they deserve. He recognises the superficial faults of *Sive* but he admits that these loom larger in retrospect than they do in the playing.

He goes on: "The reasons for the play's theatrical strength seems to me the meticulously faithful realism, the firm character-drawing, the brutally observed theme, and the emotionally effective songs of the two wandering tinkers."

Hogan stresses the realism and claims that the strongest quality of the play is the cold accuracy with which the lust for money is painted. H. L. Morrow, in an adjudication, called *Sive* "a prodigious play" and thought that the play's great glory lay in its dialogue. He said it was as "rich, as gusty and full-blooded as Synge". Jim Fitzgerald, a brilliant producer, said of the play, "The writing is thick, three dimensional. It is this rather than the melodramatic plot which is the play's virtue. The characters are inflated by the language they use to giant size . . ."

Few in Ireland will be unfamiliar with this story of a young girl forced into a marriage with an old and repulsive farmer by her greedy relations but this plot outline tells nothing of the real power of *Sive*. A scholarship adequate to its range and strength will be necessary to illuminate its full dynamic and, John, let us hope it comes soon rather than late.

In a passing reference Robert Hogan almost discovered another key factor in *Sive*. He refers to one scene in which Sive's Aunt Mena and the matchmaker, Thomasheen Sean Rua turn on the old grandmother, Nana. Hogan writes of this, ". . . it is so intensely black that one thinks of Boslola tormenting the Duchess of Malfi."

He leaves it thus but your play as a whole has mighty Elizabethan force. Your lines carry the seal of dramatic poetry and your rhetoric would not be incomprehensible to the world of Webster and Shakespeare.

In this sense your characters exist on the plane of universal representation and it provides something akin to an apotheosis of realism. Your modesty may be offended by all this but I would go further and compare *Sive* and other of your plays with the aesthetic splendour of the Japanese Kabuki and Noh theatres and the comparison is perfectly valid. The rhetoric of movement no less than of speech and the conventions of vocal force so vital to the oriental presentations are all to be found in the play *Sive*.

It can be admitted that the basic plot of *Sive* is not original but then there hasn't been one since Genesis. What is important is the fact that the treatment of the material, the dialogue and the characters add up to something epic. Although it is possible to question the suggestion that the real merit of the play lies in its realism; it must be said that you touch the pulsating and elemental heart of rural Ireland in *Sive*. In this respect you far surpass Synge and the play is absolute evidence of that superiority. His response was that of an observer; yours was that of the participant.

The towering splendour of *Sive* does not rest on any single aspect and its enormous force is derived from a cross-fertilisation of many sources of dramatic energy. It is realistic only in the sense that the imagination and the sensibility give total assent to the validity of the characters but the play as a whole is a masterpiece of stylisation. In fact it has something in common with ballet for the richness of the dialogue sweeps in graceful arabesques even when it carries a burden of savage irony and bitter greed. Ultimately it is the stylisation which lends the whole thing a universal quality.

The tinkers in *Sive* are a powerful element but they are so closely woven into the fabric of the play that they cannot be isolated from its identity. They underline your talent for musical composition and in *Sive* and *Many Young Men of Twenty* you made lasting contributions to the repertoire of the balladeer.

Pats Bocock and Carthalawn are characters in their own right and also subjective observers of the action. In a sense they have divine objectivity as they fulfil the part of a Greek chorus through comment on the action and counsel to the characters. They are amongst the most vivid creations of twentieth century Irish drama.

Had *Sive* not existed I would have lavished the same praise on *Sharon's Grave* which, in some ways, explores areas of the soul far beyond the range of the other play. It would be enough on its own to secure you a place in the history of the Irish theatre.

But then you have produced enough to furnish the reputations of a dozen writers and your creative extravagance outpaces comment. There are so many other plays which offer an array of characters unequalled outside Dickens and one thinks of *The Highest House on the Mountain*, *Many Young Men of Twenty*, *The Man from Clare*, *The Year of the Hiker* and the sombre horror of *The Field*

Looking over them again one is struck by the tragedy of your isolation from what at the moment purports to be The National Theatre. This is a grave loss to both and one despairs of those unidentifiable elements in Abbey Street.

Your short stories have been given the recognition they deserve. *Death Be Not Proud* for example is a chilling, callous tale that somehow produces a resonance in the heart of every Irishman.

In it one feels the urgency of the harvest as the rain storm threatens and when Mikey Henderson's mother dies in the fields the reader may be horrified to give assent in imagination to the decision of the man and his father to press on with the work. You too may endorse the thought of Mike Henderson as he looks at his son, "Beyond doubt here was a man with a sound sense of values, a man with a true feel for the land."

Later, John, the reader may question his conscience but in the immediacy of the literary experience the necessity and logic of the moment is accepted due to your remarkable craftsmanship and verbal magic.

Most people do not associate you with the novel and yet you have written five or six which are certain of enduring fame. You must be aware that the famous series including *Letters of a Successful T.D.*, *Letters of an Irish Publican*, *Letters of an Irish Parish Priest*, *Letters of a Matchmaker* and the rest belong to the genre of the novel. The letter as a device for story-telling was common in eighteenth century fiction and it was used often enough in the nineteenth. I stress this, for the coherent and structured fabric of your Letters has not been sufficiently recognised.

But it is not merely that each novel captures the ambience of its central character and exploits all the humour of situation and character he or she offers; there is the total community which is depicted in the Letters as a whole. The Parish Priest, the Publican, the Matchmaker and the rest are all focal points of social power. In effect you have created from rural Ireland something akin to Balzac's *La Comedie Humaine.*

There is tragedy, poignancy and sentimentality in the Letters, John, but forgive me if I recall the hurricanes of laughter that blow from their inspired pages. I think of Dicky Mick Dicky O'Connor's aphrodisiac suggestions to Mrs. Snoss; the wild and agitated cry for help from Peadar Lyne in *Letters of an Irish Publican* and the hilarious wisdom of Father Martin O'Mora, P.P.

And your essays, John, your essays! What a switch in style these represent. In general they are urbane, sophisticated and polished even when they deal with the most earthy topics. But you've done so much and done it so well.

You are an honest man, John, and a modest one and so you may imagine that all of this is no more than a load of flattering codswallop. But you do have reason to know that I am sincere and your family of books may also persuade you to accept that you are something rare and something unique.

You are still relatively young and I have a hope that maybe the best has yet to come but you've nailed down your claim to a high place in the history of Irish letters even if you never write another line. And you will write more . . . a genius of your like never gives up and you have something above and beyond talent. As someone once wrote, "Talent repeats; genius creates. Talent is a cistern; genius is a fountain."

Many years to you, John, and the success you deserve and may the fountain of your inspiration never run dry.

Yours sincerely,

Tony Butler